Unchained
Value

Unchained Value

The New Logic of Digital Business

MARY J. CRONIN

Harvard Business School Press
Boston, Massachusetts

Printed in the United States of America

04 03 02 01 00   5 4 3 2 1

Library of Congress Cataloging-in-Publication Data

Cronin, Mary J.

Unchained value : the new logic of digital business / Mary J. Cronin.

p. cm.

Includes bibliographical references and index.

ISBN 0-87584-937-7 (alk. paper)

1. Electronic commerce.   I. Title.

HF5548.32 .C76 2000

303.48'33—dc21   00-031911

The paper used in this publication meets the requirements of the
American National Standard for Permanence of Paper for
Publications and Documents in Libraries and Archives Z39.48-1992.

To

Scott B. Guthery

Done with the compass.

Contents

Acknowledgments

Every book is the product of countless discussions, interactions, and points of view. When the topic is the intersection/of business and the Internet, the number of relevant inputs goes up exponentially. My work on *Unchained Value* drew inspiration, examples, and insight from that richest of all sources, the Internet. The list of online collaborators, interviewees, and e-mail correspondents is too long to detail, but I gratefully and continually acknowledge the generous contributions of information and insights from Internet-connected managers around the world. Without them, this book would never have taken shape.

Closer to home, my colleagues at Boston College's Carroll School of Management have been a vital source of support. To Jack Neuhauser, who was there at the beginning and remains a valued advisor, and to Hassell McClellan, for his encouragement through the graduate program, my special thanks. I am grateful to Rob Fichman and John Gallaugher for sharing their own research findings and for the many on-the-spot discussions of e-commerce and technology innovation. To Joe Jose for his tireless and inspired help with diverse research projects, and to Dave Murphy for his unassuming but essential leadership, which makes our department a productive place, my thanks.

Funding for a concurrent research project on international Web sales from the Carnegie Bosch Institute provided another important source of contacts, data, and company site visits that helped to support and enrich the examples in this book. I appreciate the support of Michael Trick and Cathy Burstein in bringing the project to a successful close, and for putting me in touch with valuable management resources.

The ideas behind this book have been germinating almost as long as there have been commercial transactions on the Internet, but a more proximate inspiration was certainly my work with many Internet start-up companies over the past few years. In particular, I thank Steve Bayle, John Connolly, and Peter Roden for involving me in the formative stages of planning and launching their companies, and for all our subsequent discussions of the twists and turns of e-business strategy. A special note of thanks to Erik Rasmussen for the many introductions and discussions of emerging dot-com enterprises and to Scott Alpert, Jeff Clark, and my fellow board members at the Aurora Funds for the opportunity to participate in the venture funding side of the Internet start-up experience. Thank you also to Nick Imparato, Niraj Shah, Payton Anderson, Kip Frey, Manoj George, Chris McAskill, and Ian Sutcliffe for your ideas and contributions. Multiple gratitude to Tom Anderson for double duty as a front-line e-business practitioner and presenter. May his own books multiply and prosper.

I owe more than gratitude to Hollis Heimbouch at Harvard Business School Press for her unstinting encouragement and faith in this project and for her contributions both personal and editorial. She has made *Unchained Value* a better book in countless ways.

Finally, my endless thanks to Rebecca and Johanna for being exactly who they are.

C H A P T E R   O N E

Beyond the E-Commerce Comfort Zone

Everyone agrees that the Internet economy is creating unprecedented value for those companies that harness its global growth engine, even as it turns many of today's leaders into also-rans. The billion-dollar question is how to build an enterprise that really does move, grow, and produce profits at Net speed. Masters of the Internet will become the titans of the twenty-first century. Companies that can't make the transition to creating sustainable digital value will struggle just to survive the decade. These are unavoidable facts facing traditional firms and dot-coms alike. The Internet is forcing everyone into a new race where the stakes are unlimited and the rules are still in formation. No one can afford to sit it out, and it has become clear that this contest will be a marathon and not the short dash that some had anticipated.

Focusing on long-term value generation should provide some much-needed advantage to the well-established firms that have traditionally specialized in surviving economic shifts with endurance in the stretch, rather than rapid bursts of change and innovation. But even though a number of the early dot-com sprinters have in fact dropped out of the race, the world's largest corporations have been curiously unable to capture the rewards of the Internet economy.

Whether measured by revenue growth or increased brand loyalty or expanded market share, traditional companies as a group continue to lag behind their rhetorical embrace of e-business.

Even managers who seem to be doing all the right things to implement online programs are finding it difficult to keep up, much less forge ahead. Competitors with new business models are grabbing market share, customers armed with online information are driving harder bargains, and product and pricing strategies are under siege. Most frustrating of all, it is hard for executives to crystallize what specific strategies are propelling the Internet leaders to success.

This book analyzes two major issues that are central to the future direction of the Internet economy. First, why has it been so difficult for the world's largest corporations to leverage their existing strengths and resources to establish a clear advantage in the electronic marketplace? Second, and closely related, what are the key competencies that allow much smaller online enterprises to reap the rewards of the Internet economy so rapidly and effectively? Addressing the first issue calls into question the structures and strategies that are deeply embedded in established companies across all industries. Answering the second illuminates the differences between sustainable digital advantage and overnight success stories that are likely to flash and crash. Understanding the answers is essential for every company that intends to stay in the e-business race for the long term.

In the past, corporations prospered by mastering a set of business processes and practices organized around the most efficient movement of goods from raw materials to finished products to sales outlets. The Internet economy has made this type of corporate organization a liability instead of an asset. The complex, integrated back-end systems that large corporations spent years to build and millions to maintain are giving way to modular, networked applications that deliver better performance for a fraction of the cost. The IT infrastructure that used to differentiate multinationals from small- and medium-size enterprises and create competitive advantage is well on the way to being commoditized as high-powered vertical marketplaces provide end-to-end online trading, distribution, and supply chain management services that are open to all. To make sense of the welter of e-opportunities, managers need to develop strategies and processes that reflect the new realities of the electronic marketplace.

This book proposes a radically different way of integrating online processes and relationships, based on replacing the traditional value chain with a digital value system.

The strategic building blocks of this new value system are not inbound logistics and operations management, but are focused on managing the information and relationships that underpin all activities in the digital economy. The five critical elements of a digital value system are information, trust, real-time relationships, customized services, and e-marketplaces. Until these five elements function as a coordinated whole, even the most aggressive e-commerce practitioners will not be able to keep pace with the needs of customers or the shifting competitive landscape of the digital economy. Bringing them together in the global electronic marketplace is powerful enough in its own right to change our way of thinking about products and profitability. The interrelationship among all five creates a continual, dynamic interchange of information and digital value—information about individual preferences that pushes products to the next stage of development and can be shared with suppliers, vendors, and distributors to motivate top performance despite pressures on time and price; and value that can turn browsers into buyers, keep customers coming back for more, and attract business partners who will move with increasing speed to meet explosive demand. By combining these building blocks into a digital value system, companies will accomplish the following:

- become faster in analyzing and acting on the massive quantities of information generated online;

- actively earn and safeguard customer trust by providing visible value with every interaction;

- consistently advance online relationships into partnerships for mutual advantage;

- augment products with flexible online services whenever and wherever they can enhance productivity; and

- effectively differentiate themselves in the electronic marketplace.

Far from discounting the importance of bricks-and-mortar infrastructure, we argue that unless established companies bring these five building blocks into alignment, the value of their current infrastructure will decline and they will be unable to compete effectively. The ultimate winners will be those companies, large and small, that unlock the value they are already creating within their own organizations and multiply it millions of times over by aligning their interests with Internet-based partners and customers in a digital value system. To do so, they must break their ties to outmoded business processes and first-generation e-commerce programs—a step that is significant for any size organization and understandably more difficult for the largest and oldest companies. This book challenges managers to look beyond the day-to-day demands of today's electronic marketplace to confront the long-term impact of the Internet economy on every aspect of their business.

Unchained Value will lead you to understand why an apparently successful e-commerce program can turn out to be your company's worst enemy and to figure out where you stand in the transition from a traditional value chain organization to a true e-business. Most of all, *Unchained Value* will give you a whole new perspective on what it means to manage a business on the other side of the digital divide, where information, trust, relationships, and services form the core of a value system that can match the speed and growth of the Internet itself. We start by analyzing the problem that companies face in translating their tangible assets into online advantage, a problem that is rooted in industrial-age models. We then look more closely at the strategies that traditional companies and dot-coms alike must adopt to successfully launch a digital value system.

Stuck on the Value Chain

The world's largest corporations have always had a peculiar relationship to the Internet. During the early 1990s, the formative years of the commercial Net, early adopters outside of the computer and technology industries were few and far between. The unprecedented global popularity of the World Wide Web in the second half of the decade brought a dawning realization that the Internet was a business force to be reckoned with, as well as an essential IT tool. Nevertheless, multinational managers were still reluctant to commit their companies to online transactions. As late as 1998, only about 39 percent of retailers and 15 percent of manufacturers were actually selling any products on the Internet.[1]

The e-commerce tide rose quickly, however, and by the end of the decade, it was clear that the electronic marketplace would be a central source of future profits and growth. By 2000, the previously skeptical majority of corporate giants had been converted to e-business rhetoric if not practice. Goaded by the skyrocketing stock valuations of dot-coms, Global 1000 executives were suddenly looking for ways to reinvent themselves as Internet companies. This fervent public embrace of "e-everything" by corporate leaders was a transient phenomenon as dot-coms started to drop by the wayside and a dose of reality hit the stock market. But the widespread inability to follow through on this rhetoric with successful digital business models has more complex roots.

As Lou Gerstner, chairman and CEO of IBM, noted in a *Business Week* opinion piece, "I was recently with the highly regarded chief executive of a major U.S. multinational who admitted to me that he has told his executive committee: 'Do something with the Internet—anything.'... Something strange is happening here. Major businesses all over the world are starting to act in some very unbusinesslike ways. And many CEOs have an air of desperation about them."[2]

The rapid roll out of Internet programs announced by many large companies does indeed seem to be driven as much by desperation as by true e-business innovation. Managers reaching for a convincing Internet strategy consider acquiring unproven dot-coms or spinning off core business resources with speculative business models. Somehow, managers have come to take for granted that smaller companies have the best long-term chances for success in the Internet economy. But this is a strange assumption given that most Internet ventures are still losing money, paying exorbitant amounts for branding and customer acquisition, vulnerable to any downturn in stock valuations, and generally living on the edge. Compare this to a typical Global 1000 corporation that has established brand recognition, a solid customer base, multinational distribution channels, and a track record of profitability, and it would seem that the advantage belonged to the long-time leaders. Except that these large corporations are clearly still stymied in their search for an effective way to leverage their enormous assets on the digital playing field.

Their efforts to date have been less than impressive. The Gartner Group projects that at least 75 percent of the e-business projects currently underway at large companies will fail within two years.[3] Gartner attributes the problem to poor management planning and unrealistic expectations about how well Internet-based technologies will interface with legacy IT systems. There's no question that managers need to take a critical look at their current Internet direction. But it will take more than revised project plans that break away from business as usual to turn a traditional corporation into a successful digital contender.

Unchained Value argues that the problem with e-business preparedness goes a lot deeper than a need for more careful planning and technical readiness. The more fundamental issue is that the strategic models and competitive tools that most managers reach for instinctively—the models that are deeply ingrained in the very structure of their companies—are the wrong maps for the digital world they are attempting to negotiate. As a result, these companies are woefully unprepared for the demands of real-time, online business on a global scale. Corporate structures and legacy systems that have taken shape over several decades do not adapt gracefully to many aspects of the online economy, and there is no magic wand that can transform those structures automatically. Applying the same competitive strategies that created today's corporate giants to the totally different demands of an e-business environment is like trying to run the Boston Marathon wearing ice skates. At the heart of the Not-Com Paradox is this—the processes that large corporations developed to rule the Industrial Age have become barriers to their adoption of Internet-based systems. The infrastructure and IT solutions that have been central to every corporate process are now weighing them down at the same time that the online equivalent of such solutions has become readily available to any new competitor.

Inside the organization, the ranks of corporate managers are far from giving up on the business models that have generated profits and increased productivity for their entire careers. It's true that leaders in every industry are dedicating an ever-growing slice of their IT budgets to Internet initiatives. But these online programs often end up consolidating current practices instead of transforming them. The financial motivation for e-business adoption is also problematic since shifting to digital business models can cannibalize current distribution channels. It is hard to justify repeated multimillion-dollar investments in programs where the most immediate impact is likely to be a decline in traditional revenues. When it comes to a shrinking bottom line, many executives draw back from dramatic transformation and settle for incremental changes.

The new logic of digital business requires a totally different framework for managing businesses and measuring success. The Internet creates its own universally accessible electronic marketplace, linking manufacturers and service providers directly with suppliers and customers, thus subverting the flow of goods and services through existing well-established channels. Instead of a predictable sequence of processes that is controlled from within the firm, companies must juggle multiple simultaneous relationships to deal with a wide variety of outside organizations and with the volatile demands of their own online customers. These factors make the traditional distribution channels and operations infrastructure liabilities instead of the means to gain competitive advantage.

For companies trying to accelerate to Internet speed, the traditional value chain has become more of a ball and chain. Almost everything about the Internet economy runs counter to the value chain model that serves as the backbone of today's largest companies. Front-line managers have to devote as much or more attention to partnerships and players outside of the firm as to internal processes. In fact, the Internet rewards companies that are skilled at outsourcing or renting applications to manage everything except their customers. This model of organization allows rapid growth, but it multiplies the number of interactions and relationships exponentially. Processes are open and shared among numerous participants, including customers. What were previously tightly integrated inward-looking activities are now dynamically linked to the firm via networked information flows not under direct control. The Net enables its participants to take advantage of unprecedented speed and scale, and in fact demands they do so.

In the traditional value chain, the marginal value that is generated inside a single firm (from the difference between the costs of the activities and the price that the market will pay) creates incentives to reduce interactions to the minimum necessary for production and to optimize through standardization and efficiencies of scale. The more people who are involved in a process, the more expensive it becomes and the less margin it generates for the firm. This drives large corporations to consolidate and reduce the number of suppliers and business partners in the interests of efficiency rather than overall firm effectiveness. In sharp contrast, digital value is cumulative. The more suppliers who join an online marketplace, the more valuable that marketplace becomes for all participants. Most e-commerce initiatives, however, do not take full advantage of these forces and the online processes that enable them.

Instead, as the next section discusses, corporations attempt to preserve existing processes by creating an e-commerce comfort zone that melds the old way of doing business with an Internet interface. This simply delays the inevitable confrontation with emerging e-market forces.

E-Commerce inside the Box

By taking this approach, executives are creating in-house versions of e-commerce that will not threaten core corporate lines of business or revenues. Rather than moving all procurement activities to the Web, suppliers may be linked to an existing proprietary system. Selected products are sold online, but not the high-margin items that carry different price tags in different countries. Decisions about joining a third-party or competitor's e-marketplace are passed from one management level to the next.

Companies can implement supply chain management, Web sales, online customer service, and many other stand-alone Internet programs and still remain well within the bounds of existing business models. This range of activities is broad enough to keep managers fully engaged in solving the immediate IT, integration, and policy issues that any Internet program will present. The boundaries of the comfort zone tend to be invisible from within the organization, where it appears that every step is breaking new ground and where short-term results receive close attention.

The drawbacks to this incremental approach to e-commerce become apparent only over time—perhaps when an Internet-based competitor has managed to attract a significant market share based on a truly digital business model. The positive benefits that often accompany early-stage e-commerce efforts all too often mask problems and trade-offs within the organization that will prevent a transition to digital value. When managers try to move on to more advanced strategies, such as developing Web-only products, launching broader e-markets, or spinning off parts of the business into stand-alone dot-coms, they discover that they still lack critical components and expertise for those endeavors.

E-commerce programs that are stuck inside the comfort zone share some tell-tale characteristics. These include the following:

- The company launches its public Web presence without changing any of its core processes.

- Costs of the Web implementation and related activities are written off as "learning experiences" and seen as unlikely to be justified by online revenues in the foreseeable future.

- E-commerce managers do not have authority for other lines of business or broader strategic responsibilities within the organization.

- Publishing pricing information for all products online is seen as a major strategic risk for the company.

- Prices and speed of delivery/support are typically tied to traditional business processes and can't compete effectively with dot-com alternatives.

- Online activities are vulnerable to skeptics and downturns within the larger company—there is pressure to cut back or pull the plug on e-commerce programs when performance in the traditional business is lagging.

The more of these characteristics that a company exhibits, the less ready it is to compete head on with true digital business models. Instead of taking advantage of the Net, companies becalmed in the comfort zone are likely to find their managers are making tactical decisions that are sensible for the short term but ultimately become detours on the road to digital value. These companies are often skilled at using the Web for marketing and branding or for specific applications such as customer support. Nevertheless, they shy away from challenging established industry channel and revenue models. John Hancock Insurance, for example, embraces the Web for consumer marketing and has won awards for the design of its public Web site. Hancock invests heavily in an interactive marketing and online banner campaign that personalizes its online messages with information geared to different stages in the customer life cycle for buying insurance. But its business models still protect the insurance broker channels and draw the line at adding direct consumer sales or comparisons to other insurance resources to its site.

Warner Brothers Records also provides an advanced public Web site for marketing and even for electronic commerce. Warner's top recording artists are featured, interactive chat rooms are available, and a shopping cart for CD purchases of Warner labels recordings is easy to use. What's missing on the Warner Web site and in its e-commerce program is any mention of downloadable content in any digital sound format, despite the fact that this technology is revolutionizing the way that music moves across the Net.

Compaq Computers is well known for its strategy of working with resellers and supporting the concept of channel distribution for its products even after Dell, Gateway, and other direct online sales started to make inroads in the PC market. While Compaq spent precious time trying to convince its resellers and distributors to make better use of the Net, Dell captured market share with shorter turnaround times, lower prices, and Web-based build-to-order manufacturing strategies. Compaq's attempts to move gradually into a limited direct sales model on the Net met with firm resistance from resellers, and Compaq was forced to revert to a channel-dominated distribution model, which hurt its sales and long-term growth potential as well as its market valuation.

In the retail realm, many market leaders waffled on Internet sales until they were confronted by strong virtual competition, and even then failed to act decisively. Toys 'R Us executives held back on direct Internet sales even though its early Web site entry and strong brand recognition made it a popular online destination for wired kids. The initial e-commerce strategy that aimed to provide synergies with its stores via a gift registry and kiosk program quickly fizzled. When the rapid growth of eToys and other Web toy sites started to threaten its market position, Toys 'R Us finally decided to spin off a separate online division with venture backing from Benchmark Partners. But the deal fell through when it became clear that the Toys 'R Us board and top executives were still more interested in protecting store sales than in having the premiere online site for toy sales.

Every one of these corporations, and all the others that have not transcended the e-commerce comfort zone, can cite countless internal constraints and external risks to justify their position. But sooner or later, executives will confront a difficult choice between preserving current business practices (and the revenues they generate) and abandoning those practices in favor of the digital alternative. If the choice doesn't come from within the corporation, it will be forced on management by the competition or customer attrition. A company that cannot escape from the comfort zone because it is still tethered to a traditional value chain will then spend a lot of money to enter a contest it has no chance of winning. More agile competitors will swarm past such companies, and even if most Internet-only ventures run out of steam, at least some of them will be strong enough and well-funded enough to stay the course.

Internet-focused companies understand that their options are to win big or to go under fast, and that understanding propels them to keep advancing and adjusting right along with the capabilities of the electronic marketplace. When their first attempt doesn't work out, they have no option except to adopt another business model and expand their network of partnership as quickly as possible. This drives a constant push for innovation and reinvention that is an important characteristic of business on the other side of the digital divide, the territory that we will explore in the next section.

The Digital Divide

On the other side of the digital divide, reality is moving closer and closer to the theoretical model of a perfect marketplace as new online exchanges take shape and achieve critical mass. The Internet provides buyers and sellers with unlimited information access, easy price and quality comparisons, the elimination of middlemen, fierce competition among suppliers, and unprecedented customer bargaining power. Not all the elements are in place in every industry, but the basic components of digital exchange are gaining momentum.

While well-established businesses are struggling to straddle the gap between their bricks-and-mortar foundations and this digital frontier, the dot-coms have raced ahead to claim vast expanses of online territory with business models that are tailored to a totally connected world. But there is a razor-thin edge between soaring and crashing in the Internet economy, and dot-com executives are even less at ease than their bricks-and-mortar counterparts. Net entrepreneurs face unrelenting pressures to turn promising concepts into sustainable revenues and to keep ahead of the next wave of brasher, faster, and even hungrier upstarts.

Even a multibillion-dollar market capitalization cannot bullet-proof a company that loses its competitive edge. As Amazon CEO Jeff Bezos is quick to point out, today's e-business models are very much in flux, and it is far too early to declare victory: "I don't want to give the impression that our future success is assured. I believe the opposite. I believe our success is not assured. If you look at the history of pioneers, it's not good."[4]

Managers don't need to consult their history books to concur with Bezos that the e-business landscape is littered with landmines. They already know that the odds are against them, either from watching failed attempts to translate bricks-and-mortar processes into Internet profits or from tracking the rise and fall of early e-commerce ventures. For every dot-com that rockets to a billion-plus valuation, there are thousands that crash and burn along the way. It is essential for managers to be able to look beyond the factors such as aggressive venture funding for Internet-based start-ups and volatile market valuations for dot-coms and to understand the sustainable advantages of a digital business model.

Over the past few years, dot-coms have managed to turn many long-held financial models on their heads. New Internet ventures have achieved astronomical market capitalizations with unprecedented speed and have elbowed their way onto the lists of the world's largest companies. Not too long ago, it would have been completely impossible for executives and analysts to imagine that an Internet search engine such as Yahoo! could expand so quickly to become a new media star worth more than the combined market cap of the Big Three automakers. The Net seemed to disrupt the classic formulations of profitability and return on investment (ROI) along with everything else that characterizes multinational corporations and their firmly rooted assumptions and modes of operation.

The dot-com halo effect has already slipped, however, and even the hottest Internet-based companies must address issues of profitability and value generation. Managers who are committed to the centrality of online business and the competitive requirements of the electronic marketplace can guide their companies to make the leap. Executives at Charles Schwab, for example, saw during 1998 that the company's newly established eSchwab online trading division was tempting customers away from its higher priced services and unsettling the brokers in its bricks-and-mortar locations. After some internal debate, Schwab bit the bullet and reoriented the whole company toward online trading, slashing the price of in-person trades from an average of $69 to a single, Web-competitive price of $29.95. The result was a short-term hit to revenues and market valuations, as the average price of a transaction plummeted. But within twelve months, the number of trading accounts at Schwab had doubled from 3 million to 6 million, and the company had established itself as a leader in Web-based investing services.

Technology companies have been leading the charge for digital business, not least because they are selling the solutions that other enterprises need to make the leap. Cisco and Dell have moved the majority of their sales and customer services functions to the Web, transforming their business and revenue models in the process. Oracle and HP adopted the banner of e-services and are working with distribution and application services partners to change the way that companies can purchase and access their products over the Internet. Egghead Software took even more extreme measures, closing down its retail stores and laying off most of its employees to become a pure dot-com, selling and distributing software via the Web. Even the icons of the Industrial Age, the automobile manufacturers, have adopted the role of digital change agents, embracing Internet-based supply chain markets and aggressively pursuing the Holy Grail of customized build-to-order sales models.

Willingness to bet the business on the digital economy is the price of admission for moving beyond the e-commerce comfort zone, but not a guarantee of success. What enables some companies to make the leap into the digital unknown while others cling to the ledge for as long as possible? The key factors include the following:

Support at the top. It takes conviction and consistent leadership from the top executive positions and the board of directors to drive the type of change required, especially given the predictable negative short-term results. A strong leader mandates change and inspires confidence that it will work. General Electric is a good example. CEO Jack Welch has added to his reputation for forward-looking management by insisting that business managers devise a "DestroyYourBusiness.Com" strategy within every division at GE. It may be mostly rhetorical, but top-level attention pushes the whole company's thinking to beyond the e-commerce comfort zone.

Long-term perspective. As the Schwab example shows, the immediate results of bet-the-business strategies may be mostly bad news. Schwab's revenues and share prices took a hit in the first year, then rebounded to new heights. When conpanies open up direct online communications and sales to their customers traditional channel partners are likely to push back. Managers need a long-term view to make it through this transition phase.

Cross-industry and market outlook. The best opportunities for growth may well be outside of the current customer base and possibly in another industry altogether.

Strong organizational buy-in. Charles Schwab's president and co-CEO, David Pottruck, led a symbolic walk across the Golden Gate Bridge to mark the transition from the old Schwab business structure to eSchwab. The message was clear—every part of the organization was making this trek together. In contrast, even though Merrill Lynch's belated embrace of direct trading on the Net seems designed to cut back on revenues for traditional ML brokers, the company did little to promote buy-in by members of this group. Every one in the company has to understand the reasons for adopting an aggressive online stance.

Extended and scalable network infrastructure. As dot-coms quickly discovered, when your critical transactions take place on the Net, if your Web site goes down, you are out of business. If there are any weaknesses in the corporate IT infrastructure, the time to fix them is before shifting business across the digital divide.

Willingness to relinquish control. Executives have to let customers and business partners play a decisive role in shaping their online businesses—even if these outsiders make recommendations that may be counter to the prior practices of the parent company. Even more broadly, the type of control that large corporations are used to exercising is not compatible with the pace of business development on the Internet.

The digital divide is not a single line in the sand. It is a constantly moving target that requires companies to keep accelerating at Internet speed. Even as managers become more willing and able to cannibalize their former business models, there will always be another, even hungrier predator out there somewhere on the Net getting ready to pounce. It is not enough to compete with one's own past; companies also need a strategy for dealing with a constantly evolving digital future. That is where a digital value system can provide a new and more reliable compass.

Forging a New Value System

This book pushes beyond the limits of short-term e-commerce implementation to help managers develop a strategy that will move their companies into the next stage of digital enterprise. It addresses a profound shift in how corporations will achieve productivity, profitability, and competitiveness in the era of the Internet. *Unchained Value* takes a new look at how companies are struggling to adjust to digital competition and analyzes what has gone wrong for those in danger of being left behind for good. It provides a framework for how to organize a business that draws sustainable energy and strength from the Net in order to unlock the full extent of previously untapped digital value.

Chapter 2, "The End of the Chain," reviews in more detail the limits of traditional value chain models in developing effective strategies for e-business. It makes the case that simply improving current business processes and partnerships via the Internet offers diminishing returns in an online world and highlights the key business process transformations that indicate a shift from the old economy to the world of digital business.

"Launching a Digital Value System" in chapter 3 describes the core elements of a new approach to developing e-business strategy—one that harnesses the characteristics of the digital world to generate new value instead of struggling to redesign and constantly speed up current processes.

Controling the information about business processes and customer preferences has become more valuable than the physical processes themselves. The advent of automated processing and data networks and the increased complexity of modern business have increased the flow of information generated from transactions and online data exchanges to a torrent that overshadows the capacity of most businesses to turn that information into appropriate action. The Internet has unleashed this flood of information at the same time that it has escalated the requirement to make decisions faster and more accurately than ever. Chapter 4, "Information: The Purest Form of Value," explores the different levels of online information collection, sharing, and analysis that underpin digital value generation and describes how companies are successfully mining this self-renewing resource.

Information is the first essential component of a digital value system. Trust is the second. And trust is arguably the least understood and most commonly misapplied element of online strategy. Many managers confuse trust with security and assume that once high-powered security tools and infrastructure are in place, user trust is bound to follow. Chapter 5, "The Dynamics of Digital Trust," makes a clear distinction between implementing security, defined as "preventing the wrong things from happening," and building the trust needed to support innovative online services and relationships—"ensuring the right things happen." This chapter demonstrates how companies build value, solidify relationships, and open the door to new types of services as they move from specialized to generalized applications of online trust.

The Internet transforms the nature of business relationships and the role that managing relationships needs to play within the organization. More cross-currents and interconnections are possible, and they are harder to control. As chapter 6, "The Power of Exponential Relationships" explains, the Net makes relationships more complex, multi-directional, and volatile at the same time that it offers unprecedented opportunity to translate online interactions into ties that will strengthen over time. Online companies have to provide incentives to become the nexus for as many relationships as possible—this is what defines the scope and growth capacity of any digital value system. Chapter 6 analyzes the need to get beyond the transactional and instrumental basis of relationships to leverage the unique power of the Net.

The Internet is hastening and enabling the final stage of a long-term economic shift from manufacturing and selling products to providing value added services. Chapter 7, "From Commodity Products to Customized E-Services," analyzes the opportunities for innovative, individual service delivery on the Net. Increasingly, the brokered economy will drive down the prices of basic manufactured goods and will turn first-level digital content into a free online deliverable. The key to profits in all sectors will be to provide new value through follow-up services, the more customized the better. To be effective and to sustain profitability while building customer loyalty, such services will have to be launched from a base of real-time, trusted, information-rich relationships. Otherwise, the attempt to extract service opportunities becomes disruptive and distracting to the other business functions.

Chapter 8 moves inside the brokered economy to analyze the impact of the trend toward online brokerage and dynamic pricing in every industry sector. As more goods and services go up for bid on the Web, every company will be forced to reevaluate long-standing assumptions about pricing strategies and product positioning. Is there a viable business case for giving away products to attract service and subscription revenues? This chapter examines the risks and competitive forces unleashed by a perfect electronic marketplace and looks at the business models of companies that have emerged to take advantage of it.

The external demands of dynamic pricing and real-time value generation require a very different type of organizational structure within the firm itself. Divisional boundaries that created clear lines of command over key activities in the old-style value chain have become barriers to essential cross-communication. What can companies really achieve with a digital value system? The final chapter, "Maximum Digital Value," prepares readers for the next stage of Internet business development, the emergence of wireless commerce.

The ticking of the Internet clock presents some urgent and intractable issues for companies that are still straddling the line between traditional business processes and the online economy. Increased reliance on the electronic marketplace is likely to jeopardize relationships with current channel partners and revenues. The costs of e-commerce initiatives tend to accelerate much faster than the immediate bottom-line savings or productivity gains. Integration of online systems with existing IT infrastructure is more complex and time-consuming than anyone predicted, and the skills to develop advanced e-business applications are in short supply. On the Web, the competition for online customers is fierce, and the rules of the game appear to be in constant flux.

The pressure to change and adapt is never-ending. No matter how quickly established companies push to integrate the Net into their organizations they seem to be outpaced by the start-ups. No sooner had corporate Web sites launched a serious effort to attract visitors than the heavily trafficked, free search engines and community sites became portals and grabbed control of browsing patterns. Just as those same companies began experimenting with selling selected products via the Web, industry-oriented information aggregators became "infomediaries" and started offering one-stop shopping for business buyers. The rapid rise of virtual competitors in every industry and the galling fact that these Internet-only companies have in many cases achieved market recognition that challenges the well-established industry leaders have set off corporate alarm bells.

Making the transition from a controlled and predictable value chain orientation to the chaotic world of open and unlimited access to digital value by all players can be expensive, disruptive, and risky. For some companies it may seem next to impossible. What happens when the short-term gains have been harvested and every part of the value chain has found its online analog? When business processes and infrastructure are stretched to capacity and the demand for more, faster, cheaper just keeps accelerating? That's the point where most managers run into a brick wall and where strategies based on traditional value chain models become counterproductive. That is the point where most e-business books end. That still-contested terrain is where *Unchained Value* picks up the story.

CHAPTER TWO

The End of the Chain

Henry Ford had it easy. He had to invent only one major business breakthrough to launch an industrial empire. And he didn't have to worry about competitors selling more colorful, cheaper imitations of the Model T at some globally accessible online auction house. Today's CEO has to cope with a tidal wave of innovation, a shrinking half-life of products, competitors offering free alternatives, and a customer who expects to dictate the terms of purchase. In retrospect, the challenges of the Industrial Age seem straightforward.

If corporate life before the Internet was not simpler, at least it sometimes slowed down long enough to let managers catch their breath. The structures implemented to enable mass production had remarkable staying power. The assembly line and other industrial innovations have long since been superseded by information technology and pervasive networking. But for much of the twentieth century the model of a large corporate infrastructure fine-tuned for production, a labor force segmented by function, and a hierarchical management system retained considerable influence. With various industry-specific adjustments and technology-driven changes, this model shaped fast-growing companies in consumer goods, in computer manufacturing, and even in financial services. The division of responsibilities and organization of business processes into a rational progression from the purchase of raw materials to manufacturing, marketing, sales, distribution, and customer service that characterized large firms came to define the very nature of the modern corporation across all industries.

A deep-seated consensus about these organizational essentials has survived various waves of innovation-minded management theory, from horizontal structures to reengineering and virtualization. Fundamental production processes have absorbed several generations of computerization and network technology. Along the way corporations have certainly become flatter, denser with information, and more interconnected, but many traditional structures remain intact. Within this framework, the design and implementation of basic business operations and their perceived relationship to efficiency and profitability have also established a compelling hold.

The Classic Value Chain

A powerful argument for using these core business functions to obtain competitive advantage was developed by Michael Porter as part of his groundbreaking work on competition in the 1980s. To indicate the scope of his model, Porter notes, "Every firm is a collection of activities that are performed to design, produce, market, deliver, and support its product. All these activities can be represented using a value chain. . . . A firm's value chain and the way it performs individual activities are a reflection of its history, its strategy, its approach to implementing its strategy, and the underlying economics of the activities themselves."[1]

The approach of organizing companies around separate business units played an implicit role in corporate organization throughout most of the twentieth century. Porter provided a methodology for analyzing all of the interdependent activities that are common to basic business processes and for using this analysis to understand how organizations can achieve competitive advantage within their industry. With widespread adoption of Porter's comprehensive strategic framework for all facets of business activity, the notion of a central value chain has been deeply ingrained in corporate managers' strategic thinking and planning. Over the past two decades, it has inspired countless theoretical and popular refinements and has shaped how large corporations go about developing long-term business strategy and short-term tactics for competing on a day-to-day basis. So why should managers finally break free from this model and substitute a markedly different Internet-based framework for business strategy?

There are three compelling reasons to leave the traditional value chain behind. First, the explosive growth of the commercial Internet has created a thriving digital economy where the old assumptions about the best way to manage logistics, operations, distribution, and customer service no longer apply. Second, the forces that are driving this growth require a new set of core competencies that are focused outside the boundaries of the firm. Finally, the competitive landscape now favors those firms with dynamic and flexible networks of relationships and "just-in-time" infrastructure access that can scale to meet surges in demand from millions of global customers. This ability to move and respond at Internet speed is an essential component of digital advantage. Unless established companies replicate this type of flexibility and responsiveness, they cannot hope to cross the digital divide and compete in the Internet economy.

The classic graphic representation of a business value chain pictures the firm's major activities as a tightly integrated chain of arrows, flowing in a logical sequence from bringing materials into the firm to the sales and support of finished products. The model extends to include the company's related support activities such as overall firm infrastructure, technology development, human resource development, and procurement along with the relevant value chains from suppliers, customers, and other business partners. Porter's original value chain definitions, as summarized in *Competitive Advantage*, include the following:

Inbound logistics: Includes all the activities required to bring the inputs for creating the product under the control of the firm.

Operations: Includes all the activities that the firm undertakes to create its final products, from actual manufacture to testing and packaging and the operation of the facilities where these activities take place.

Outbound logistics: Includes all the activities required to get the product into the hands of buyers, from materials handling and warehousing to processing, scheduling, and delivery.

Marketing and Sales: Includes the activities involved in selling products into a market, from advertising, pricing, and promotion to developing channel partnerships and deploying direct sales forces.

Service: Includes all after sales activities required to maintain and support the product.[2]

Like the engine at the heart of the Model T, this fundamental model of corporate structure absorbed and adjusted to repeated technological innovations and improvements, evolving to keep pace with the times as computers, networks, and back office information systems became essential for global competition. The transition from mass production to mass customization to micromarketing leveraged the rapid development of information technology without disrupting the core assumptions behind the model. When corporate managers adopted technology to optimize every stage of the business, from supply chain management to distribution and service, models of the value chain expanded right along with technology. Over the past ten years, the original value chain framework has been stretched and expanded to accommodate the notion of virtual companies and other networked organizations. It has been adapted to the global network as the "internet value chain" with a focus on making business processes more efficient by moving them to the Web via intranets and extranets.[3] Recognition of the differences between bricks-and-mortar exchanges and online relationships generated new models for a "virtual chain" based on networked commerce.[4] These variations on the original value chain model helped to provide a bridge between traditional business processes and the interactive networked environment.

The Chain Breaks Apart

As long as the underlying economic assumptions about industries and competitive environment remained valid, the classic model provided a resilient combination of structure and flexibility. Now, however, those assumptions are less and less relevant to the realities of business on the Internet. Instead of stable relationships with suppliers and distributors, companies face constant flux. Electronic online markets make information about pricing and product availability that used to be closely guarded within the firm accessible to all—partners and competitors alike. Customers don't wait patiently to receive the finished products that emerge from the end of the chain—they expect those products to reflect their personal input and to participate in their production from the moment of order.

The more companies within an industry begin to develop strategies and products for the Internet economy, the less relevant the traditional value chain becomes. A point-by-point comparison of the classic value chain definition for each core business process with those same processes transformed in the online world helps to bring these differences into sharp relief.

The capsule summaries of the changes in assumptions and key business goals that follow highlight the fundamental shifts in each area.

Logistics

Moving logistics and supply chain management to the Internet has had a dramatic impact on the speed and efficiency of contracting with suppliers for raw materials and expediting those materials or components through the operations and outbound logistics cycles. Now the entire process may be managed via the Web, starting with dynamic auction markets bringing together buyers and suppliers to set price and delivery options in real time. With firm online agreements in place, companies can authorize direct shipment of raw materials from suppliers to an assembly point (often outsourced as well) or a succession of component and manufacturing partners, each of which will complete its designated steps in the assembly process. One result is a blurring of the distinctions between inbound logistics, operations, and outbound logistics, as the responsibility for procurement, assembly, and distribution may shift among a number of online players. The customer-facing company may be simply an online entity with no physical presence in terms of manufacturing and warehousing of goods or may be an original equipment manufacturer using the Web to establish direct customer relationships.

The increased popularity of Internet-based marketplaces and exchanges for business-to-business materials, combined with the spread of dynamic pricing, has already forced buyers and sellers alike to rethink their logistics and distribution strategies. Every industry has sprouted one or more e-marketplaces for the online procurement of raw materials and the disposition of new, used, and surplus goods. These exchanges are slated to grow dramatically over the next several years, with IDC predicting that Web-based procurement will double in size every year.[5]

In addition to the impact on fabricating durable goods, the shift from atoms to bits has an even more dramatic effect on the end-to-end processes for software, financial, and other sectors that offer digital products. Many of the basic activities covered in a bricks-and-mortar value chain model don't apply at all to the transfer of digital goods and services. No need for warehouses and packaging plants when information-based products can be downloaded directly on demand (see table 2-1).

Operations

Getting better control of operations inside the firm has been a long-term business process focus. Within every complex organization there are processing redundancies, information bottlenecks, and various barriers that get in the way of drastically reducing the time between order and fulfillment. Reengineering efforts and IT investments in enterprise resource planning (ERP) systems during the 1980s and 1990s were aimed at streamlining and rationalizing end-to-end operations within large corporations. But the performance improvements and time reductions

Traditional Economy	LOGISTICS	Internet Economy
"Inbound" goods and services to be assembled are under the control of the firm.	*Assumptions*	Components are acquired and assembled in response to real-time customer demand.
"Just-in-time" approach locks in most favorable cost and delivery terms with selected vendors.	*Goals*	"Anywhere, anytime" ability allows contracting for materials as needed to ensure efficient assembly and delivery.
Materials handling, storage, inventory control, transport.	*Critical Activities*	Managing information and scheduling to accommodate build-to-order strategy.

Table 2-1 Shift of Assumptions and Goals of Logistics from the Traditional to the Internet Economy

that resulted were often disappointing—the processes themselves remained more or less intact, and the costs involved in implementing the ERP cure often outstripped any benefits that could be measured.

Despite, or perhaps because of, the huge investment that many large corporations have made in installing massive ERP systems over the past decade, these companies are woefully unprepared for the demands of real-time, online business. A preoccupation with ERP system implementation has been at least a distraction and in many cases a definite barrier to Internet adoption. It typically takes several years to implement a supplier information system based on ERP models, and it is not unusual for Global 1000 companies to spend well over a billion dollars implementing a full-scale installation. But even after this massive effort, companies are far from ready for the Internet economy. Many of these installations fail to live up to their original goals of internal integration and productivity boosts.

Even when ERP programs do succeed at improving performance and increasing the efficiency of operations within the firm, these benefits are limited. Results of a 10 percent improvement in cost savings or productivity are considered acceptable; results of a 20 percent or better improvement are at the top of the scale. Most companies don't ever

Traditional Economy	OPERATIONS	Internet Economy
Internal efficiencies are essential to reduce costs and accelerate cycle time.	*Assumptions*	Ability to scale and produce on Internet time requires outsourcing to strategic partners.
The focus is on establishing best practices in key operational areas.	*Goals*	The focus is on establishing "best partners" for outsourcing as many functions as possible.
Process design, assembly, packaging, equipment performance, facility operations, managing of ERP systems.	*Critical Activities*	Building to fulfill customer orders and continual scannning of broader markets to develop new offers ahead of pent-up demand, managing of ASP solutions.

Table 2-2 Shift of Assumptions and Goals of Operations from the Traditional to the Internet Economy

complete an entire firmwide ERP implementation. Less than 5 percent of the companies that have implemented one ERP module go on to integrate their entire infrastructure. One of the reasons for dissatisfaction with ERP installations is that they tend to perpetuate existing processes, creating a giant and inflexible system. What companies really need to be successful on the Net is innovative, real-time customer management systems and a robust back-end switching engine that can keep multiple partners and customers up to date about fluctuations in product demand, price, fulfillment, performance, and all the other details that are responsive to external requests (see table 2-2). The ERP systems are inward-looking at a time when a large part of the most important action and information is available only outside on the Net.

In contrast, Internet-focused companies are managing their operations and linking with the core business processes of partners, suppliers, and customers by "renting" operations management software and other applications as needed from application service providers (ASPs). As chapter 7 discusses in more detail, the growth of ASP solutions is propelling new business models for traditional companies and dot-coms

Traditional Economy	DISTRIBUTION	Internet Economy
Substantial time and space are required for physical handling and warehousing of goods between manufacture and final delivery.	*Assumptions*	Minimal time is needed between product completion and delivery to end customer.
Efficiencies in in-house storage and delivery systems.	*Goals*	Build-to-order capacity and streamlined inventory.
Inventory control and ability to schedule delivery based on demand.	*Critical Activities*	Establishment of trusted information channels and partnership relations.

Table 2-3 Shift of Assumptions and Goals of Distribution from the Traditional to the Internet Economy

alike. The ability to access high-level software as needed makes it possible for even small companies to track complex interactions and modular operations and to scale as quickly as necessary to meet demand for products and services without being tied to an expensive IT infrastructure.

Distribution

The Net has transformed the distribution models for both physical and digital products. The Web provides a new window on the demand for goods and the best match between products and markets. Business partners can see directly into each other's inventory and order databases, and adjust distribution schedules accordingly, cutting back on unproductive shelf time and costly rush deliveries (see table 2-3).

Now companies with a direct, continuous connection to their customers can avoid the costs and risks associated with inventory storage and make profits on far thinner margins. The most telling example of this advantage has unfolded in the computer industry, where manufacturers with long distribution chains are continually thrashed by fluctuations in price and customer demand and rapid upgrade cycles, which can make inventory obsolete. Compaq and IBM cannot compete effectively when companies such as Dell move to shorten their internal operations and take advantage of the Web to process orders direct from customers and then to coordinate information and order transfer between all component suppliers. The savings are enormous—an order of magnitude factor that makes it possible for Dell to continue discounting its products without losing its margin and to grow as quickly as customer demand warrants without maintaining expensive inventory on its own. No industry can afford to have a blind spot between its operations and its customers; the traditional channels have been a black hole with too little feedback too late to change production and development cycles.

Marketing and Sales

As more companies begin to understand the power of the Internet to reach individual customers, the amount of money spent on advertising and online marketing programs has skyrocketed. But the tactics of buying banner ads and tracking Web visitors are still rooted in traditional marketing concepts that are centered on the firm rather than the customer's perspective. Developing truly customer-centric and personalized marketing campaigns requires stepping outside of the value chain mentality (see table 2-4). Chapter 6 discusses in more detail how the Internet supports new forms of personalized and customer-controlled campaigns and viral marketing programs where word about products spreads rapidly from online referral and community-building networks. The community sales model pioneered by Amazon and widely imitated by other online merchants illustrates the power of partnership in a networked environment. Amazon sales associates now number in the hundreds of thousands.

Service

The traditional company also has difficulty keeping up with the varied support requirements of its customers. Depending on the type of

Traditional Economy	MARKETING/SALES	Internet Economy
Customer choices within product categories are limited; firms can use positioning, product quality, and pricing to differentiate themselves.	*Assumptions*	Choices are infinite, and feature-by-feature comparisons are inevitable; customer online experience is a key differentiator.
Convince the customer.	*Goals*	Empower the customer.
Advertising, direct sales, channel management.	*Critical Activities*	Provision of value-added interactive experiences and building of trusted online relationships.

Table 2-4 Shift of Assumptions and Goals of Marketing/Sales from the Traditional to the Internet Economy

product, after-sales support and service can require a completely separate unit or outsourcing arrangement. Many traditional support and service programs provide little feedback to the development and operations departments inside the organization about product features that are causing support problems or suggestions from individual customers about potential improvements or new products. Service is provided on a "one-size-fits-most" basis, which inevitably leads to overloaded call centers, long waiting periods, and unhappy customers with little value added for either party in the interaction.

The self-service capabilities of the Internet have provided well-documented cost savings over traditional support and service programs. By letting customers help themselves to information and problem resolution resources on the Web twenty-four hours a day, seven days a week, companies are able to support a rapidly growing customer base with a much smaller investment in staffing and call centers. Even more important is the fact that well-designed Internet-based service actually increases customer satisfaction, especially when integrated with access to personal help via Web chat or telephone.

Online service can also be as varied and individualized as necessary. One customer may want certain types of products to be personalized,

Traditional Economy	SERVICE	Internet Economy
Firm is on call for products that need repair; field service teams for high-end installations are needed.	*Assumptions*	Continual contact with customer to make products more intelligent over time is crucial.
Satisfy the customer.	*Goals*	Capture lifetime customer loyalty.
Enhancing or maintaining the value of the product.	*Critical Activities*	Maintaining online support and service information plus interactive diagnostics and solutions, providing remote network access to "smart chips" in every appliance and product.

Table 2-5 Shift of Assumptions and Goals of Service from the Traditional to the Internet Economy

while the next is interested in direct delivery of modular product components for do-it-yourself integration, while a third (or three millionth) just needs to download a more detailed product description and wants to do it right now (see table 2-5).

Ramping Up Digital Processes

Any one of the process transformations just described is large enough in scope to have a disruptive impact on the way that business is conducted inside the typical firm. Put them all together with the explosive growth, rapid pace of development, and innovative applications that characterize the Internet environment, and the disruption becomes a major revolution. Now, any company can help itself to the information resources and communication capabilities that used to differentiate the largest companies. Online firms of all types can provide the personalized attention and services that used to be the province of the specialty high-end firms. And they can do all this while optimizing the speed and efficiency of production and distribution through ASP services and multiple Internet-based channels and partnerships. Companies can no longer look at their competitive advantage in terms of a well-integrated value chain that holds these forces together because what really counts today is what is happening outside of their immediate reach.

Breaking the links of the old value chain does not mean neglecting the issues of integration and fulfillment or acting as if logistics and service don't matter in electronic environments. Far from it. These capabilities matter more than ever, and one of the fatal flaws of bricks-and-mortar–oriented value chains is that they cannot deliver what it takes to be successful in the world of e-business. As many companies have learned, excessive traffic can be worse than hackers at shutting down Web sites and disrupting customer service. When millions of users hit the send button at the same time or when hundreds of thousands of unique orders flood into a patchwork IT system that was designed to handle a few hundred regular customers, things can fall apart quickly and visibly.

The whole point is that the Net requires totally different performance and scale from corporate fulfillment and back-end systems. Systems that were designed for predictable and stable links between all the parties responsible for separate functions, from the input of materials to operations, production, distribution, sales, and support, will not survive the digital value test. The back-end requirements are unforgiving. Does the order get through? Are suppliers and distributors aligned and able to scale to demand? Does accelerating online demand spell disaster or dollar signs? Are customers able to get the information and the product in whatever way they want it? These are the make-or-break questions about any business process model, and they apply equally to dot-coms and bricks-and-mortar companies. Many dot-coms, in fact, focus their attention on building brand and perfecting the front-end interactions with customers and neglect the nitty-gritty details of fulfillment and integration among multiple partners. The results are negative.

Start-ups, even technically savvy ones, are not immune to problems such as Web outages and fulfillment crises. These were common during the first wave of e-commerce demand in the pre-Christmas 1998 shopping season. With inventories depleted, busy signals rampant, and customers losing patience, online merchants vowed to prepare for the best-case traffic scenarios during Christmas 1999. Nevertheless, traffic-related problems persisted for many Web sites that faced record numbers of visitors and floods of orders that overwhelmed undersized systems and fulfillment planning. The Internet makes three inexorable demands on companies interested in harvesting its value-generating potential—speed, scale, and size. And it punishes any company that can't keep up the pace.

Consider the bumpy ramp-up of Handspring, Inc., the company that aims "to transform ordinary organizers into customizable handheld computers." Founded in July 1998 by the creators of the wildly successful PalmPilot product, the company generated considerable advance publicity and demand from devoted Palm customers well in advance of its first product rollout, the Handspring Visor. Its marketing literature and Web site promised the ultimate in handhelds—a sleek, cheap, user-friendly platform that could morph into a digital camera, an MP3 music player, a wireless communicator, and much, much more.

The promotion stirred expectations that the first-generation Visor would be one of the "must-have" products of the new millennium. The game plan seemed well calculated to capitalize on the advance publicity and to piggyback on the popularity of the PalmPilot by selling directly to consumers via the Web in the fall of 1999, before making the Visor available through retail outlets. The reality of the situation points out the pitfalls of under-powered Web sites and the need for Internet-strength back-end systems. The Handspring Web site announced that the Visor was available for sale and promptly sunk beneath the weight of high browser traffic and more orders than it could handle. During the crucial pre-Christmas 1999 season, the site was down more than half the time. To make matters worse, customer files were lost in cyberspace because of a glitch in transferring files from the ordering system to the fulfillment and shipping databases. Putting up a toll-free order number only made things yet more frustrating—the systems were still error prone, and callers spent most of their time waiting on hold. Some customers got duplicate shipments while other orders were left unfilled because of mix-ups about priority. The resultant confusion swamped the customer services area— so instead of cheering on the surge in customer interest, Handspring had to engage in what its head of sales called "demand suppression."[6] That at least gave the company some time to tune up its back-end integration and database operation and implement some basic Web sales features like real-time updates on customer order status. But it was far from the instant success story it could have been and definitely not the "small, simple, and connected" image that the company wanted to project with its product debut.[7]

Handspring management was able to rebound from this rocky beginning during 2000 and began to leverage the positive response of customers and reviewers that did get their Visors. But their experience illustrates that dot-coms and traditional companies alike are hard pressed to keep up with the inexorable forces of the Internet's demands for scalability, unless managers put the building blocks of the digital value system to work. Many dot-coms, caught between traditional value chain limitations and under-powered Web systems, will not get a second chance. But as the following examples illustrate, there will be no respite for established industry leaders. The next wave of Internet-based competition is positioning itself to take full advantage of digital alternatives for every link in the value chain.

Forging Digital Links for New Business Models

A brief look at two very different industries, insurance and automobiles, underscores how quickly the Internet-based companies can move from formation to execution of models that bypass existing value chains.

Compared to online stock trading and investment services, the largest U.S. insurance companies have been moving in slow motion to adopt even the most basic e-commerce capabilities. But the established insurance companies can't hold back the tide of digital competition much longer. Many segments of this $800 billion industry lend themselves to online distribution. The product itself is information-based, and each individual policy reflects a series of conditions and decisions that vary from customer to customer. It is highly regulated, with each state setting a somewhat different set of requirements. That means that researching all the options for even one type of insurance coverage and matching requirements with coverage plans and prices are complex and time-consuming processes—ones in which each new piece of data can change the recommended product. These are all problems that lend themselves to the personal profiling, database mining, self-configuration, and search capabilities of the Web.

There are other ways that the Internet can add value to both insurance providers and consumers. The purchase price is typically high, and there are lots of opportunities for cross-selling to satisfied customers, making it worthwhile to invest in the up-front marketing and high-end interfaces that work best to present complex information products on line. Many customers could simplify their lives by filing claims online or initiating routine information updates such as change of address, providing an opportunity to reduce the insurer's overhead costs and enhance customer satisfaction. That has been a winning combination for the computer hardware and software industries.

If the insurance industry were being created from scratch today, the Web would certainly be the centerpiece of its marketing and delivery strategy. But the solutions that emerged well before the availability of the Net rely much more heavily on separate channels for distributing the complex information. Providers have set up elaborate networks of individual agents to help potential customers sort through layers of options to customize a policy that matched their personal needs. The state-based regulatory structure made it important to have large numbers of fairly knowledgeable people based in different geographic locations. It was enormously expensive to support such a large and dispersed staff as salaried employees, so the approach of selling insurance through independent agents who made hefty commissions from each policy sold and provided all the needed hand-holding at the local level made market penetration and expansion much more feasible. Hence, the complex, large-scale, and still powerful channel of insurance agents—U.S. companies alone employ almost 200,000 of them. This channel adds dramatically to the cost of every policy sold: sales costs for the same policy are more than $100 via an agent and less than $10 via the Web. In addition to inflating the cost of every policy issued, this channel now stands in the way of large companies leveraging the full power of the Net.

Insurance company Web sites are plentiful, but they offer their customers little beyond basic brochureware and prescripted planning scenarios. Of 3,000 U.S. insurance Web sites surveyed in the summer of 1999, fewer than 1 percent provided the ability to actually purchase a policy directly. Existing customers had little opportunity to file claims or receive personalized policy information online. Even companies that positioned themselves as leaders in implementing e-commerce were struggling to reassure the agent channel that online initiatives would bolster agent-customer interactions rather than eliminate them.

In short, this is an industry that appears ripe for Internet inroads. The incumbents are large, entrenched in inflexible value chain relationships, and slow to take advantage of online alternatives. There will be market and channel resistance, and the industry leaders are unlikely to feel much impact yet, but this is another case where the Web will inevitably win. Smaller competitors will offer insurance sales via the Web, personalization options will improve, agents will adapt or go out of business, and the Internet will become a dominant force in the industry. There are already more than 300 dot-coms in the United States involved in some aspect of insurance sales. Only a few have to make it big to transform the habits of the insurance buying public forever.

eCoverage

Internet-based eCoverage doesn't make a secret of the fact that it is taking on the insurance giants full tilt. In fact, the battle plan of this online insurance provider is written on its sleeve. The tag line on eCoverage's Web site proclaims, "The Industry is History." That slogan may be irreverent and overambitious coming from a start-up with no track record in the insurance business, but it speaks volumes about the aspiration to become a catalyst for transformation in an industry that has resisted change from within.

The founders of eCoverage recognized their inexperience in the insurance industry, but they were determined to launch a venture that could make a quick impact in a major industry sector, and they saw insurance as an appropriate target. Their start-up strategy was to attack the old-line, integrated, and very cross-subsidized automobile insurance industry.[8] eCoverage zeroed in on automobile insurance in California as a starting point. California auto insurance was typical of the national model. Consumers bought insurance from intermediaries and had little control over the price they had to pay or access to comparative information about carriers and coverage options. Plus, the state offered a large enough market to make the initial effort to meet state regulatory requirements worthwhile.

The eCoverage management team aimed to move the entire auto insurance channel onto the Web, from marketing to underwriting to describing options and policies to the processing of claims. They saw the company as being a full-service provider—not necessarily competing on the lowest cost basis, but modeling itself after a Charles Schwab or eTrade. Their ideal was to be known as a full-service discount insurance provider, a company that made it easy for customers to help themselves. They saw that their advantage would come from using the Web to offer end-to-end services and to build a direct relationship with the consumer. They could then use their information about customer needs to provide extra value-added services and to keep improving the online experience for every stage of the insurance process.

The founders concluded that speed to market with this new type of service was much more important than building and controlling an IT and Internet infrastructure from scratch. They decided to outsource as many functions as possible, even though this was not always the most cost-effective approach. Instead of worrying about the long-term economics of the business at the start, they theorized that having a first-mover advantage was better than a balanced budget projection. The assumption of the founders and their investors was that eCoverage would figure out a model for profitability when they were up and running and had a chance to sort through the overall business opportunities more carefully.

The critical path to first-mover advantage was getting licensed to sell auto insurance via the Web in California. This meant establishing a legal entity that was entitled to underwrite and bind policies online. It was clear that eCoverage had to outsource the underwriting function to an established insurance provider in order to acquire a critical mass of customers and industry expertise in one step. Online acceptance and processing of all claims was another area that required specialized competency and therefore was a good candidate for outsourcing. In fact, the only thing eCoverage was adamant about controlling directly was the overall customer relationship, including support and follow-up services. As long as they maintained this direct link to the customer, the rest of the business could be handled by insurance-savvy partners. In order to ensure quality and build relationships with the customers, the management team structured the outsourcing relationships and information flows so that eCoverage staff could monitor all customer contacts and address any problems with customer service that might occur.

With initial funding in hand in the summer of 1999, eCoverage founders raced to become a fully operational player in the auto insurance industry in twelve months or less. After just three months dedicated to signing on partners and service providers and establishing their base of operations, they were able to open the doors on a Web site and start to write California auto insurance policies with thirty-five staff members. Six months after that, they had expanded to selling insurance in four other states and were ready to move from automobile coverage to additional insurance categories, such as homeowners and boat coverage. That timetable may be unthinkable for the large industry leaders, but it is typical of how aggressive online ventures tackle their chosen markets. The next goal for eCoverage is to double its size and begin to build a nationally recognized brand. Additional alliances, including an agreement to offer its services through Auto-bytel's car-buying Web site, are already drawing national attention and customer queries.

In essence, eCoverage has unchained the process of selling insurance policies by substituting stand-alone partners and IT outsourcing for dedicated channels and in-house systems. By focusing on the direct customer relationship and post-sale service opportunities, they hope to harvest additional value from every customer, while accelerating the customer acquisition process and reducing its cost significantly. If this model succeeds for auto insurance, there are few barriers to extending it to other forms of insurance.

The Virtual Auto Dealership

In the automotive industry, the dynamics are different, but the ability of new online entrants to upset the existing value chain and establish a beachhead with consumers are just as significant. As with insurance, traditional channels and processes have become a barrier to implementation of direct digital sales in the largest auto manufacturers. In this case, the leading auto giants are almost universally eager to use the Internet to open up more direct connections to the buyers, but the automobile dealership franchises have been trying to keep the brakes on Internet sales. Even with all the will in the world, the automakers are cut off from direct sales on the Web by the limitations of their traditional customer-facing value chain.

Unfortunately for the U.S. makers, the current distribution channel of independent car dealerships has a strong and legally enforced hold on the franchises for direct sales, which the dealerships have no intention of ceding to the manufacturers or to the Web without a fight. Over 22,000 car dealers in the United States are protected by franchise agreements and state regulations. When Ford and other manufacturers have tried to purchase these dealerships as a step toward direct distribution and Web sales, the dealers protested so strongly that manufacturers quickly backed off.

A closer look at the automotive industry demonstrates how the chains that bind traditional industry leaders reflect imbedded business models more than technology barriers. Since Henry Ford's day, auto manufacturers have aggressively deployed technology to cut costs and cycle times. It used to take months for a particular model and make of car to go from a particular batch of orders to the assembly line to the distribution center to the local dealership and finally into the garage of the new car buyer. U.S. and Japanese manufacturers have invested heavily in IT infrastructure in order to set up systems for supply chain management and the integration of key suppliers into the assembly schedules. Use of "just-in-time" delivery of parts from suppliers connected to automotive networks managed to shave that time lag from months to just a few weeks—tantalizingly close to the time frame needed to emulate the more advanced "build-to-order" model of the computer industry. Toyota, in fact, has touted its ability to deliver a built-to-order automobile within a five-day turnaround time.

Build to order would provide the ultimate in online direct sales advantage for all the auto manufacturers. To circumvent the restrictive agreements with dealership franchises that prohibit such direct sales, each company is working though some indirect strategies to open more online channels. Ford has established a partnership with Priceline.com to accept bids from Priceline's customers and redirect them to dealers. GM is setting up direct sales Web sites in Asia where it does not have the same limitations on dealer agreements as it does in the United States.

While the auto manufacturers are locked into a distribution system that puts power in the hands of local dealerships, start-ups are courting online buyers and signing on partners to establish new digital value systems. The stalemate between manufacturers and dealers provides a vacuum that Internet-based ventures are eager to fill. Early online entrants such as Autobytel and CarPrices.com have positioned themselves in between the manufacturers and the dealerships, providing car information and comparison shopping services to consumers but ultimately referring the prospective buyer to an existing bricks-and-mortar dealership to consummate the purchase.

CarPrices.com, for example, is working to create a hybrid model by partnering with existing dealerships. Its Web site combines a now familiar online automotive shopping guide and price/feature comparison capability with software that lets potential buyers construct the vehicle of their choice by combining available manufacturer options. Then CarPrices forwards the specifications to its network of dealerships, giving them twenty-four hours to bid on price and a firm delivery date. Buyers have to close the deal themselves, based on the list of responses. The popularity of this type of service has squeezed dealer profit margins as more and more consumers do their research online first and approach dealers with a quote in hand. But the dozens of online comparison pricing and dealer referral Web sites don't target the automotive distribution model itself. Another contender, CarOrder.com, however, aims to "disintermediate" auto dealerships by moving the entire distribution model to the Web. Like eCoverage, CarOrder wants to make the traditional industry model a piece of history.

Founded by twenty-three-year-old Brian Stafford in Austin, Texas, CarOrder bills itself as the first Internet "e-dealer."[9] It has a powerful and well-capitalized parent company in Trilogy, the Austin software and integration firm that has already spun off PCOrder. With over $100 million in initial funding in September 1999, CarOrder had the resources to back up its plan for buying as many as 100 low-profit dealerships around the country and to begin using them as distribution points delivering autos that are sold via a central Web site. CarOrder is counting on lower costs and drive-up delivery to convince customers to buy from its Web site rather than from a traditional dealership.

With so much riding on its online presence, CarOrder had to get the customer interface just right from the first click to the final push of the buy button. They have succeeded in creating a Web site that is rich in information and graphical presentation of makes and models without sacrificing download speeds and response time. The customer can conduct preliminary research on different cars or get right down to the business of getting a price quote on an exact model and set of options. If customers want the reassurance of talking directly with a service representative it is easy to switch from online mode to phone interaction at any stage. And they can also investigate and arrange auto loans from the CarOrder Web.

Auto dealers who are counting on the lure of the test drive and the persistence of current car-buying habits predict that Web-based sales will never attract the mainstream consumer. But CarOrder.com is already ringing up Web-based sales, with over 2,000 new car sales a month by the end of 1999 and ambitious plans for national expansion. It seems clear that the pressure from automakers on the one side and Internet ventures on the other will break the dealership lock on the auto distribution chain sooner rather than later.

Both eCoverage and CarOrder are creating direct customer relationships and speeding up service delivery by cutting out traditional channels. Their business model assumes that successful online operations require multiple partnerships that are linked together via the Internet. Their competitive advantage, and ultimately their profits, come from aggregating these relationships and the information that they generate into value that they can deliver back to the customer.

The long-term prospects of eCoverage, CarOrder, and other startups that aim to disrupt traditional value chains matters less than the simple fact that there are thousands of such companies targeting business processes in every industry. The important question for market leaders is not whether parts of their existing value chain will give way under this onslaught—this is inevitable. The real challenge is defining the core business that will create competitive advantage in the future and moving quickly to grow that core into a digital value system.

Conclusion

The transition from traditional value chain models to a digital value system challenges established corporations and new ventures in different ways—the former must rethink existing processes while the latter are racing to amass enough customers to achieve profitability. Even though Internet-based companies have been faster off the mark, it is not too late for large corporations to adopt their own digital value systems. The multiplicity of online relationships, the speed of data transfer, direct involvement of previously passive players, and the modularization of services and solutions have all worked together to separate information about goods flowing through the value chain from the goods themselves. Free of the chain, the information that holds the value is the key to generating revenues and gaining customer loyalty, and it can flow freely in many directions.

It is past time to shift top management attention to the core activities that are essential to create business value and generate increasing returns in an Internet economy—thus laying the basis for a dynamic and flexible value system to replace the traditional value chain. The process of creating such a system and fostering its growth and expansion is open to all. This process and the rewards of implementing it successfully are the focus of chapter 3.

CHAPTER THREE

Launching a Digital Value System

No Internet venture can expect to succeed completely on its own. More and more e-business start-ups are born in incubators, fostered by interlocking digital *keiretsu*, and launched in a network of partnerships and alliances. Like the stars of intricately constructed solar systems, the most promising of these ventures tend to move in orbits around each other and to attract a number of other enterprises into their gravitational fields as they expand their offerings. Companies that base their e-business strategy on such systems will grow faster and provide a higher rate of return to investors and stakeholders. The total business impact of the Net is magnified precisely because it enables millions of commercial and individual participants to relate to each other in ways that were previously impossible. Establishing one's place in a universe of interconnected value systems has become a key strategic challenge for all types of companies in the Internet economy.

What, exactly, is a digital value system? It is a collaborative Web-centric framework for organizing the expanding universe of networked relationships and processes. It is also a model for organizing the interrelationship of information and services within an enterprise and seamlessly connecting internal and external activities into a coordinated and dynamic strategy. A fully functional digital value system has three parts:

- a set of online relationships that accelerates growth, expands the sphere of influence, and enhances the value generation potential of all participants, while making sure that "the more, the better" works at Internet scale and doesn't degrade the quality of online performance or service;

- a structure for secure, real-time access to the information, trust, relationships, and services generated among the participants for their mutual benefit; and

- a strategy for creating recurring cycles of increasing returns so that participation provides clear and continual benefits.

Firms with strong partnerships and strategic alliances are not a new phenomenon, of course. Long before the Internet, business success required building relationships, attracting and keeping customers, and creating the best possible external support and partnership groups. Traditional corporate giants have set up elaborate networks and distribution channels to handle international fulfillment and customer support services so that they could expand quickly into new markets and compete effectively with local industries.

Participating in a digital value system goes much further than those activities. Like the Internet itself, a digital value system is different in scale and in kind from the traditional value system. It may involve hundreds of thousands of partners and millions of customers in a complex and ever-changing pattern of mutual advantage. As figure 3.1 illustrates, the relationships within a digital value system map to a pattern of organization very different from the traditional value chain or even the typical e-commerce transaction. The traditional value chain, as we saw in chapter 2, limits the flexibility of companies to forge new links among business partners and customers. Placing the Web in the center of e-commerce connections greatly

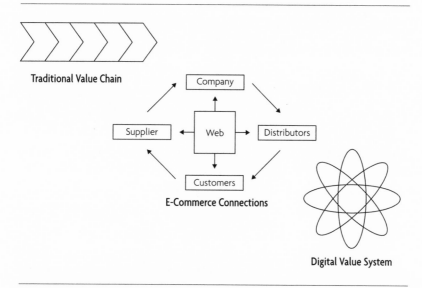

Figure 3-1 The Changing Value Structure in Business

enhances communications among all parties and creates new direct distribution possibilities. But the participants in e-commerce transactions still remain within their own separate boxes and the Internet serves as a new tool for conducting existing business rather than a totally different type of business. This configuration limits the flexibility of participants to grow at Internet speed.

In contrast, the formation of a digital value system brings all participants into constant interaction with each other. These new relationships are more complex than the traditional linear value chain or even the Web-based models, but they do create a recognizable pattern. The best metaphor for this new level of interaction is a digital solar system, where participants are in dynamic orbit around each other. As more participants join the system, the amount of information exchanged and the number of transactions completed can increase exponentially.

This chapter will describe the evolution and the infrastructure of such systems and analyze the development of the strategies behind some successful examples.

Defining Digital Value

The constant stream of online developments, new entrants, and shifting strategies comes into focus only when we stand back from the
day-to-day impact on a particular organization to consider the
broader structure of interlocking relationships and strategies and
longer-term trends. This structure gives birth to new business opportunities and spews out new threats so quickly that stand-alone organizations cannot recognize them, never mind act on them. To make
matters even more complex, the Internet has accelerated industry
convergence, turning technology companies into entertainment conglomerates and electronics companies into service providers.

In the business-to-business arena, the Internet economy has
already shifted from very focused vertical industry exchanges to more
horizontal e-market areas that are starting to bring competitors
together in one space and will ultimately cross into multiple industry sectors. Automotive manufacturers and suppliers, for example,
merged two separate e-commerce efforts that had been in place for
only a few months to bring Ford, GM, and DaimlerChrysler into a
consolidated e-marketplace. Chemdex, an early player in online markets for scientific equipment purchasing, has become part of Ventro
Corporation's integrated group of e-marketplaces serving different
industries. Starting with the acquisition of Chemdex, Ventro has
established a series of industry-focused business-to-business procurement companies that bring together buyers and sellers in Internet based exchanges. Its coverage extends from specialty medical
products through its Promedix venture to supplies in the food service
industry and in plant equipment. Each new vertical exchange brings
more buyers and sellers to the table, increasing the return on Ventro's infrastructure investment And since each industry has some supplies and equipment needs in common, participants in all the
exchanges can benefit from higher volume discounts for those items.

As Internet-based business models evolve, companies can walk
onto the digital value stage in a number of different roles, from information aggregator to community builder, from a service provider to

an online market broker. In the business-to-consumer space the most-visited Web portals, such as Yahoo! and Lycos, have added services through acquisitions and partnerships to make their sites one-stop, full-service destinations for all consumer needs. As we saw in chapter 1, the opening soliloquy matters less than the ability to extend the original value proposition into a broader system of partnerships, services, and customer loyalty. A successful growth strategy draws on all the core elements of a digital value system—the information, trust, relationships, and services that the company is bringing into the brokered economy and using to improve its internal processes.

Within the framework of the value system, the relationships are dynamic and flexible, allowing participants to pursue multiple orbits that will be adjusted as needed to a particular situation. These adjustments may be as precise as the responses to real-time bid-tracking services or part of longer-term growth cycles. As multiple organizations and individuals cluster together, the activities of each participant support and reinforce the other, and as participants interact more with each other, the value of the whole increases. It is this dynamic of increasing value that holds the system together and attracts new participants and different industry segments to its field of activities.

The structure of the digital value system may involve complex interrelationships and multiple information exchanges, but its success is measured in part by the simplicity and ease of use that it can deliver at the point of contact with the end user.

The next section analyzes how every component of the system combines to add value that was not accessible to the customer or to the company in the traditional value chain framework.

The Road to Increasing Value

The transformation starts, as we have seen, with recognizing the limits of the traditional value chain view of business processes. Chapter 2 detailed the reasons for breaking those traditional chains once and for all and substituting a digital value framework as the centerpiece of Internet strategy. In the process, it became clear that core production and distribution functions have not by any means disappeared from the business landscape. Steel, rubber, glass, and plastic still get molded into automobiles that Henry Ford would probably recognize as direct descendants of the Model T. Packages still arrive bearing books, not bits. The road to establishing a digital value system doesn't necessarily mean shedding physical assets and products in favor of a bit-only business. What counts is how your company manages to share Internet-based value with your partners and customers. Managers in all types of organizations can construct a digital value system that moves the bricks-and-mortar components of the enterprise into the Internet economy, as long as they are prepared to lay the foundations of the five essential elements—information, trust, relationships, services, and brokerage. In this section we will take a closer look at how these five elements relate to each other in a way that creates a system that can yield increasing value for all participants.

In the digital economy—and in a digital value system—the information that is behind the system and generates most of its value is recognized as being distinct and separable from the tangible product itself. Logistics, distribution, supply chain management, and operations are no longer a matter of physically counting inputs and counting outputs and getting the right part on the right truck heading to the right customer. All of these things must still be done, but they can be outsourced, chopped up into modules, or even put into the hands of the customers to manage from their own location. As long as the information keeps flowing and circulating to all the right parties, picking up more details as it moves along, managers don't have to actually see the shipments going in and out the door.

The digital tsunami has swept over the value chain and has separated information from its generator. In this case the generator is product fabrication and distribution—those activities that take place within the firm and its suppliers and partners. In the value-chain era the information needed for managing the flow was inextricably bound to the flow itself. Keeping the business on track required keeping the flow of artifacts under tight control and limiting the number of entities that could alter it. This control was necessary to optimize the core processes and thereby increase profit margins. Managers could describe their goals in clear and limited terms: Tune the inventory. Squeeze the prices. Buy in bulk. Order the supplies. Keep on schedule. Produce just in time. Manage the process by managing the artifacts.

Unfortunately, the limitations of closely guarded or restricted exchange of information led to the endless repetition and fine-tuning of value-chained processes. Cycles that are perfected within the firm repeat themselves with little variation and become embedded in systems and organizational structures. Eventually the motivation and ability to do things differently atrophies. But once information about the process manages to escape these bounds and become readily available to everyone who has an interest in the outcome of the process, it will not be long before requests for changes start to pop up everywhere. The Internet has provided a massive information escape hatch for the value that was previously locked up inside the firm. The traditional value chain can provide only limited visibility into the product pipeline and none at all into the subflows and peripheral activities that influence who might eventually buy the product and why. The company makes the product—say, a toaster—as efficiently as possible and brings it to market. The customer is offered what came out at the end of the pipeline at a predetermined price. The only contribution the customer gets to make to the process is deciding which toaster to buy.

Michael Dell, founder of Dell Computer Corp. and well known for spearheading a build-to-order system within computer manufacturing, notes that the feedback system in the traditional value chain for automobile distribution can actually lead to misinformation: "If you have three yellow Mustangs sitting on a dealer's lot and a customer wants a red one, the salesman is really good at figuring out how to sell the yellow Mustang. So the yellow Mustang gets sold, and a signal gets sent back to the factory that, hey, people want yellow Mustangs."[1]

The change wrought by the Internet started with simply introducing multiparty visibility into the traditional value chain. Because the customer was connected to the same Web as the manufacturer, the distributor, the supplier, and the storefront that were selling the toasters, the customer could begin to see how the toaster was made and then participate in tracking and perhaps influencing the process. This didn't happen in just one place, but all up and down the chain wherever an Internet connection took hold. Suddenly everybody could see over the top of their suppliers to their suppliers' suppliers and over the top of their customers to their customer's customers and back full circle. New strategies for seeing further into the pipeline and sharing the view with partners and customers provided significant advantage to companies such as Dell.

At this stage, the span of control for any given company's core value processes is extended. Production becomes much more complicated than just trying to match the rate of input to the rate of output. If everyone can see into the process and if there is value in letting those observers become active participants, then it becomes apparent that the process itself is the least interesting part of the value system. The product flow no longer carries all the information needed to manage and efficiently run the end-to-end process. What we really care about is who wants to know what information and why, and who wants blue toasters and whether those same customers are also buying red Mustangs. Or from a business-to-business perspective, we are ahead of the game if we can rely on our suppliers to accurately ship the right number and color toaster components to our assembly partners who will then ship them directly to where they will be in most demand in the coming month.

In order to keep track of all this newly available information and to put it to use effectively, we need to apply trust and relationship management to our emerging value system. Much of the information needed to manage an externally oriented value system as opposed to an internal value chain has to come directly from the participants in the system, not as a consequence of their interaction with the system. Indeed, the information needed to manage the system isn't even in the consequences. The simple sale of a toaster is just a tick in the store inventory system. No amount of computing on the prices I can get from my suppliers will tell me about the intentions of their suppliers or about their other customers. So the value system must also provide incentives for all participants to share information as openly as possible in order to function at peak efficiency. It is important to note that the incentives for business partners will be different from those that are likely to motivate end users and customers. In fact, the five key components of the new framework do not all have the same weight across business-to-business and business-to-consumer markets.

Once the information has successfully broken free from the artifacts (the message from the media), we are on our way to defining a new economy—a digital economy that requires a different kind of information-based value system. Prices, production, and the local status of the pipeline were the currency of the value chain economy. Information about the process (meta-information about the prices, production, and global status of the pipeline, if you will) is the currency of a digital economy. A digital value system lives on systemwide information. And the more quickly that information can be converted into action, the more value the system can generate. This insight provides a clear case for information pooling among all the players in the value system. Digital value participants recognize the need to move from value-chain, price-and-product local information to end-to-end, systemwide information pooling. What companies discover through participation in Internet exchanges and Web-based information pooling is that meta-information requires more and more of a less well-understood component of digital exchange, namely trust.

Business-to-business trust now underpins the burgeoning online exchanges and B2B marketplaces, but business-to-consumer trust has been a challenge to establish and maintain in the digital environment. There are a number of reasons for the missing consumer trust connection on the Internet, which are analyzed in more detail in chapter 5. It is clear that online merchants have not paid nearly enough attention to the requirements for building digital trust. Yet transacting business online requires a much greater dynamic range of trust from the customer than shopping in the bricks-and-mortar world. In the value-chain economy, remember, all that the customer could contribute or was expected to contribute was to take or not take the toaster off the shelf. In the new digital value system economy, the consumer, like everyone else in the market, is expected to contribute information that establishes the elements of that person's digital identity and becomes a valuable component of the information pool. Suddenly, purchasing a toaster seems to involve inviting the merchant into my kitchen to observe breakfast preparations. If I get some valuable assistance in return for the invitation, it may make me a customer for life. But if the merchant shows up uninvited, I may slam the door forever.

Once trust and information find each other in the proper balance, the digital value-system economy is ready to kick into high gear. The first stage of the payoff is deeper and more personalized relationships with customers and with suppliers. The traditional value chain created a dangerous blind spot beyond a company's regular market scan. Manufacturers would only find out about the run on toasters (or the failure of the new toaster oven) when stores reported sales results. By then merchant and manufacturer were both hard pressed to adapt to customer demand. The Internet has overcome the traditional trade-off between customer volume and customer intimacy. It has even gone a step beyond to bring the viewpoint of the entire connected community within easy reach. The result is faster self-correction as conditions change (responsiveness), which in turn leads everyone to be continually engaged in market-molding behavior (real-time interaction)—the R Factor phenomenon discussed in chapter 6.

The digital value system model also helps managers understand where service-based revenues are likely to emerge from the Internet economy because they are constantly interacting with customers and potential customers. The optimal outcome isn't selling out the last toaster just as demand falls to zero. That was a goal of value chain thinking. The most sustainable revenue sources are not based on products at all. They are based on service. A product sale is simply the opening bell. Providing e-services puts companies ahead in the race for recurring revenues and lasting customer loyalty.

Once again, the information is the starting point for value—the dimensions and delivery of the service must reflect accurate information about the needs and preferences of the customer, not just about the service itself. The value is in the information about who wants the toaster, what they are going to do with it, and what type of bread they are going to buy every day for the next twenty years to put into it. Once we know these things, we know when to offer which services to this particular customer. Would they like to connect the toaster to the Internet and watch it working from their computer at the office? Or does it make more sense to provide a link between the toaster and their mobile phone? The customer is now at the point of buying and valuing broader services, not simply the toaster circuitry and wires. It is the product in action—or the service—that counts in the digital economy. That's what is embedded in the information-pooled, real-time interaction bits when they are separated from the product. That's what companies need to know to make the next loop around the digital value framework faster and better for all participants.

Information requires trust. Trust begets relationships. Relationships improve service. Within this value framework, the trend toward dynamic pricing goes from being a disruptive threat to being the logical culmination of the system. Companies close the loop by participating in e-marketplaces, and the brokered economy takes another leap in speed and size and begets even more precise information. At the end of the day, the value of any given item must be determined by how much it will fetch in the marketplace. In the bricks-and-mortar world this information is painfully—and expensively—delayed by putting the toaster on a shelf with a price tag and waiting for months to find out if the price is set at the right point to move the most toasters into the most kitchens. This delayed valuation is focused on the least information-rich and least dynamic part of the system—the durable product. Once we refocus on the live, individual customer, we can bring trust and relationship back to the fore, and we can shorten the latency period and make the pricing process dynamic.

It makes sense that if my use for the toaster differs from what the rest of the world plans to do with it (both valuations of which are essentially independent of the cost of the physical object), then what I am willing to pay will be different than what other customers are willing to pay. But without a real-time feedback loop, the provider makes a best guess at the right price point and waits. The brokered economy has already established a variety of information pools in the form of e-marketplaces, from eBay to eSteel, to collect and clear the amounts we are willing to pay for any given item. Many more markets are on the way, as each industry sector develops its own digital value system.

Once dynamic pricing takes hold, it wants to spread. Otherwise, too many companies will be caught between static prices on the expense side and dynamic payment of customers on the revenue side. As long as everyone has access to a brokered option at every intersection of the value system, the scales will balance for the benefit of the most action-oriented participants, thus rewarding those who can keep moving forward at Internet speed. The digital economy's need to set price through direct market participation, which is based on individual service valuation, leads us to the flowering of the fully brokered economy and right back to dynamic information pools. The cycle continues, and more value pumps into the system with every turn.

The Parts Do Not Equal a Whole

There is more to unchaining value, however, than simply recognizing the importance of each element in the digital value system or even organizing a business around one or more of them. All five components must be implemented in balance, connected in real time, totally interactive, and constantly expanding in quality as well as quantity in order to generate increasing amounts of value for all participants in the system. Without this balance, firms and their managers will be struggling continually against the constant churn and explosive growth of the Net instead of harnessing it as a source of advantage.

Even the relatively short history of Internet business provides plenty of cautionary examples of near misses by companies that were able to master one of these core digital value elements but couldn't construct a full-fledged value system. Time Warner's launch of Pathfinder in 1994, for example, was a pioneer effort in rich information content and user aggregation. Pathfinder provided free access to leading Time Warner publications such as *Time* and *Fortune* magazines. In a period when worthwhile Web content was still a scarcity, Pathfinder received an enthusiastic user response, registering online surfers by the millions and demonstrating the characteristic "get big fast" power of the Net. If Pathfinder had acted as the catalyst for a full-service Web value system and had broadened its original scope from providing information to offering relationships and online services, Time Warner might have been in a position to acquire AOL instead of the other way around.

As it turned out, Time Warner executives were not ready to think outside of their own publishing and media context in designing a competitive business model for Pathfinder. They did not understand how to turn the Internet's positive response into new business opportunities by building and leveraging close and trusted relationships with those millions of individual site visitors. When an effort to charge for access fizzled, they experimented in rapid succession with other publishing-oriented revenue models with little success and increasing frustration. Time Warner eventually came to see the Pathfinder site as a black hole of expenses that was detracting from their mainline publication brands. In the process, they squandered not just the hundreds of millions of dollars that were poured directly into Pathfinder, but an online user base with demographics that could have launched a dozen portals. By the end of 1999, Time Warner simply pulled the plug on Pathfinder as a stand-alone site.

Like Time Warner, Digital Equipment Corporation couldn't find a way to convert the early online success of its AltaVista search engine into sustainable advantage for the parent company. Even though AltaVista won kudos for speed and scope and became a magnet for Web traffic, Digital Equipment failed to turn those millions of visits into digital value with extended services or personalized relationships. Executives agreed to spin off AltaVista as a separate entity, but never really gave up calling the shots and insisting on some sign of traditional ROI. As its managers struggled with branding and corporate control issues, AltaVista drifted, struck scattered partnership and advertising deals, and squandered the potential of its user base.

Compaq's acquisition of Digital meant that AltaVista's potential to transform traffic into significant digital value was handed off to another company that had its own problems competing on Internet terms. After making a few attempts to redesign and reorganize Alta-Vista into a broader service, Compaq executives decided to focus on more pressing problems of overall Internet strategy and handed off AltaVista a third time. It was picked up by CMGI, the venture fund behind dozens of dot-com properties. David Wetherell, CMGI's CEO, may have hoped to replicate the early success of other investments such as Lycos and Yahoo! by turning AltaVista back into a top desti-nation site for all sorts of activities. In fact, although CMGI did open doors to additional AltaVista alliances with shopping and financial services, by the time AltaVista launched these services, leaders such as Yahoo! were well ahead in the race for customer loyalty.

Another early Web sensation PointCast made it onto millions of desktops with a creative use of push technology. The PointCast software continuously downloaded or "pushed" news and infor-mation to users over the Net, appearing in the form of a screen saver with dynamic content. PointCast introduced some of the funda-mental concepts of real-time online marketing, but the company failed to extend its ability to broadcast real-time information into interactive and value-added relationships with its users. Without a solid case for enhanced productivity or personalized services, Point-Cast proved vulnerable to the problems inherent in the push model. Individual home users did not typically have fast enough connec-tion speeds to fully use its graphic interfaces, and network managers became concerned about its bandwidth requirements inside of organizations. PointCast had not built a sustainable value system for its user base and so lost its coveted spot on corporate workstations, while BroadVision and other content engines captured market share with richer and more customizable options that could be branded by sites directly.

Security First Network Bank, the Internet's first full-service online-only bank, emphasized its sophisticated security systems to encourage early Net users to entrust their money to an online account. The bank succeeded in attracting deposits from early technology adopters but quickly hit a wall in terms of growth. Executives were not able to move from implementing a trusted technology to developing more comprehensive relationships with their customers. Ultimately, the paucity of customers made it clear that Security First was not a viable stand-alone business. Bank operations were cut back, and the Security First holding company focused on selling the secure financial system to other financial services organizations—a testimony to the strength of its own underlying security system but further proof that security alone would not be enough to build lasting online relationships.

Charles Schwab, in contrast, made a conscious decision to build in the best available security but not to emphasize it as a selling point to the end user. Instead, Schwab relied on clear online information, ease of use, and integration of phone and personal support with Web capabilities, along with the high level of trust that its customers already had in the Schwab brand. The result was rapid adoption, with more than 34 percent of accounts shifting to the Web trading option during the first two years and more than $10 billion in transactions handled every day.

Peapod was out of the gate early with an online grocery order-and-delivery service in 1997. But it relied on traditional grocery partners and didn't ever generate the margin or the scale that would allow it to show a profit, especially as contenders such as Streamline and webVan squeezed it with even more personal services offerings and warehouse-based central delivery. Meanwhile, companies such as Kozmo.com upped the ante for Web-based delivery services by offering a variety of fast foods, drugstore items, and entertainment options from click to doorstep in an hour or less. Amazon, on the other hand, moved to overcome its delayed-delivery limitations by investing in the capability to deliver within one hour from online order to doorstep and trumping the bricks-and-mortar bookstores such as Barnes & Noble, which were offering "same day pick up" at the nearest storefront.

Failed ventures like Pathfinder and PointCast, and struggling ones like AltaVista and Peapod, underscore the need to supplement early mover advantage with an integrated value system. Being first out of the gate with one value component is simply not enough to retain customers and grow revenues for long-term success. In the final section we will look in more detail at three companies that are working to create digital value systems.

A Digital Value Trio

Amazon

Amazon's evolution from online bookstore to super-retailer is an often-told Internet tale, and the end point is still nowhere in sight. Its initial growth path provides a classic example of how the Net can support an emerging company's ability to launch expanding spheres of influence that can generate value for all participants. How to convince Internet users to get out their credit cards and buy anything online was by no means as obvious when Amazon opened its Web site in 1995 as it is today. Founder Jeff Bezos needed to overcome a lot of hurdles to establish the Amazon name as a trusted brand and to get early customers involved enough to keep them coming back and excited enough to spread the word. Analysis of the strategy that has kept Amazon ahead of an increasingly crowded field illustrates how all five elements of a dynamic digital value system work together and reinforce each other.

Information has played a key role in building customer interest and loyalty for Amazon. In the virtual world, the more independent information a potential customer can find to help propel a buy decision, the better. Encouraging Amazon users to write their own book reviews had the practical value of filling the information gap between an online site and the book-in-hand advantage of bricks-and-mortar bookstores without requiring Amazon to incur the additional expense of hiring reviewers or outsourcing book review content. It also created an invaluable sense of interactive community and personality for what would otherwise be one long library-like catalog. Review writers became more than just customers; they were active and loyal partners in building Amazon's cumulative information value. Consciously or not, they were drawn into the company's expanding online value system.

The design of the Amazon Associate program created even closer ties and added a new dimension of collaborative advantage. Amazon made it easy for anyone with a Web site to claim a piece of the e-commerce action. All it took was displaying the Amazon logo, linking a list of book titles to the Amazon store, and encouraging visitors to click and buy. The Amazon logo popped up on thousands, then tens of thousands, and eventually hundreds of thousands of Web sites—close to 400,000 by 2000. It was a marketing bonanza with a bonus: each of those individual Web sites was also providing an implicit stamp of approval for Amazon as a trusted and trustworthy destination. Associates got their share of the value too, receiving a commission on each sale made to a customer who entered Amazon through them. For the vast majority, that commission check would never amount to more than a small income supplement, but it provided tangible evidence of partnership in an expanding online venture.

In the early days of Amazon's growth, its ability to create mutual advantage for customers and Associates solidified the trust and the loyal relationships that supported even more information sharing and insight into customer interests. The growth of a loyal and interactive customer base and in-depth experience with a successful Associates program also put Amazon in the position to negotiate more favorable terms for increased visibility in deals with portals such as AOL, Yahoo!, and MSN.

As Amazon expands its model to encompass multiple consumer goods and services, it must leverage and sustain the relationships and trust earned over the past several years. The addition of zShops, a diverse community of small merchants under the mantle of the Amazon brand, is one strategy for expansion. Customers who have been totally satisfied with the book-buying experience on Amazon are ready to expand the value of that relationship to other offers from Amazon, and this value transfer has allowed the company to quickly achieve a dominant position in online sales for its new product lines, such as music and electronics. However, Amazon can't exercise the same level of control over the quality of products and the level of customer services from these small companies. If some of the Amazon-branded zShops dilute customer satisfaction by providing uneven service, then Amazon will lose some of the trust that it has built up, and the value circulating within the system as a whole will diminish. So why is Amazon taking this risk? It sees the need to launch another, closer set of partnerships within its value system. The zShop merchants will receive significant value from the Amazon brand and traffic, enabling them to connect with customers who would never have found them any other way. Every sale will, in turn, generate value for Amazon—directly through commissions and indirectly by keeping customers on site longer and providing even more reasons to return. The advantage of expanding the entire value system potentially outweighs the downside of having less control.

Yahoo!

The history of Yahoo! epitomizes the evolution of the Web during the past five years. Started as a labor of love, a student-designed search engine application with no plans for revenue, it has become a top portal site on the Web and a daily destination for millions of Internet users. In the process, Yahoo! has developed into a multinational corporation with instant brand recognition around the world. One of the few Web-only companies to combine hyperexpansion and acquisition with profits on the bottom line, Yahoo! posted its first profit in the fourth quarter of 1996 and has seen its market valuation rise to well over $30 billion. That puts it into a select category of dot-com blue chip corporations. Today Yahoo! is a master of information management, personalization, and special services, which can command top-dollar advertising revenues on its ever-expanding Internet holdings.

More than 32 million visitors make their way to some part of the ever-expanding Yahoo! Web site every month, and more than 20 million have registered for one of the many special services, giving Yahoo! more detailed information in the process. On the average, Yahoo!

accumulates over 400 billion bytes of data a day from all those Web visits—more information than it can currently analyze in any detail and more than enough to fuel the growth of its media offerings. What's more, Yahoo!'s core content is the Web itself, and simply keeping up with the unrelenting increase in Web pages covered by its search engine gives Yahoo! a virtually unlimited number of pages to sell to prospective advertisers, along with specific search terms.

In exchange for serving up millions of pointers an hour, Yahoo! also gets to sit on top of a constant flow of information about what Web surfers want to know and where they want to go. Yahoo! gets even deeper information from users who register for special services, and in turn that information provides extra value to advertisers who want to target their message to a specific audience segment. So behind the scenes, Yahoo! has become expert at traffic analysis and information mining. It can match the most exacting market demographics requirements and can parlay that ability into top-tier advertising rates.

Selling advertising and demographic access to the more than 3,800 paying advertisers that have active accounts with Yahoo! generates a significant portion of the company's annual revenues. But, as many other high-traffic Web sites have learned too late, advertising cannot support increasing digital value. Yahoo!'s revenue mix includes sales, subscriptions, auctions, and many other services that supplement ad income. You can get your Yahoo! e-mail account, financial information, and personalized news; make a bid on a Yahoo! auction site; or earn points making a purchase on a partner's Yahoo! storefront. Users can talk in Yahoo! chat rooms, download customized music and video offerings, and enjoy multiparty games or kids entertainment—everything you could want to keep you coming back again and again, which of course is exactly the point.

It has been standard practice for the stock-rich dot-coms to expand through buying up already established communities and integrating them, and Yahoo! is no exception. Timothy Koogle, Yahoo!'s CEO, points to the acquisition of other leading Internet companies as a strategy for Yahoo! to reach its goal of becoming the largest media company in the world: "We clearly are being consolidators ourselves.

We have purchased probably 10 or 12 companies in our life . . . we'll continue to acquire companies at the right rate. It has created an environment where we do have a highly valued currency to use to further our strategy by acquisitions and we'll continue to use that currency in that way."[2] Among those acquisitions were a deal to absorb Four11, the free Web mail company, and its 1 million subscribers in 1997 for $93 million and to integrate all of GeoCities, with its millions of individual Web pages at a cost of $4.5 billion in 1998. Despite some initial friction with the user communities, both buys brought a substantial boost in traffic, which in turn increased ad revenue and the number of regular visitors. The purchase of Broadcast.com brought new technology and expertise in Web-based audio and video and launched Yahoo! Digital and Yahoo! Broadcast Services, which currently supports eight streaming video stations and a partnership with EMusic.com to sell MP3 downloads and broadcast audio selections.

On the surface, this is not very different from the strategy that other high-powered Web portals have pursued over the past few years. Lycos, for example, has kept right up in the acquisitions department, buying the Tripod home page community and Angelfire e-mail and directory services, along with financial services and gaming companies to bulk up its user numbers, and adding the Sonique music broadcast capabilities to help launch Lycos Music in 1999. In Web site traffic and number of services offered, Lycos is doing its best to keep abreast of Yahoo!. In one of the most critical measures of digital value, however, Yahoo! has a clear advantage. According to the Web rating service, Media Metrix, the average Yahoo! visitor spends more than an hour every month doing something on the site, while the average Lycos user spends only seventeen minutes, showing a clear difference in the depth of the relationships and the use of personalized services.

Creating a base of customer relationships and services from customer information is a multistage process. Inside the organization, the ability to track online behavior and interests and to map these to specific user demographics and buying patterns is an extremely powerful tool.

Trust encourages users to sign up through Yahoo! or any Internet company for special services, such as free e-mail, personalized news reports, and financial research, based on registration. The more trust, the more users are likely to sign up for advanced and more highly personal services and the more alienated they could become to find out that the information they had shared was being circulated to businesses and partners downstream. In Yahoo!'s case, the growth of its brand recognition and its strong presence in other countries make it now one of the world's most trusted brands. That in turn makes new service offerings, whether they be for mobile phone connections or for financial advice or stock trading, more attractive. Yahoo!'s success in rolling out these diverse services demonstrates the value of balancing detailed customer information with respect for customer privacy. The more personalized a site is and, therefore, the more an individual has invested in setting it up, the more likely loyalty and trust will continue to build.

Yahoo!'s ability to leverage the initial search engine contact into a cascade of individualized services that attract a loyal group of regular customers is even more impressive when compared to the performance of some of its early search engine rivals. Adding new member services and interconnecting all of them provide a platform for future growth. In building a cascade of value, from information to trust to personal relationships and customized services, Yahoo! has been able to convert size into value on a constant and increasing basis.

eBay

Yahoo! got its start as an online information guide with no clear-cut commercial goals. In contrast, eBay aimed to be a high-growth business from day one, but its plan for turning small consumer auctions in collectibles or recycled goods into large-scale, multimillion-dollar markets was far from obvious. Who would pay good money for unbranded, used stuff they had never seen from someone they had never met—and do it over a medium still notorious for its security issues? An Internet-appropriate component of trust needed to be built into the process.

To launch its digital value system, eBay started with relationships and a solution for building digital trust, then accumulated a store of information and a expansive cluster of services. Trust is the universal digital lubricant—lose it and any online business model will grind to a halt. Capture and grow it to become the value center of many related businesses. eBay's ability to create a new trust model for auctions via a public rating scale enabled a whole new form of online business. With that trust in place, the firm has turned into an extremely efficient electronic brokerage that handles over two-and-one-half million new auctions and 250,000 new items every day. Fifty million auctions have been completed on eBay since the first electronic gavel sounded in 1995.

On a typical day on eBay, buyers and sellers are pouring over bids for more than five million items offered up for sale in over four thousand categories. The eBay community in 2000 encompassed more than six million registered users who log onto the site frequently, generating more than 1.5 billion page views per month. Even more important, those users tend to take their time browsing and bidding. "Stickiness" ratings put eBay close to the top in terms of how long the average user spends on site every week. In June 1999, users averaged more than 111 minutes a week looking around, giving them an even higher relationship factor than highly "sticky" portals such as Yahoo!, and a massive edge over the majority of Web sites. This combination of high trust plus high relationship value has already paid off handsomely, giving eBay a market valuation of $30 billion and a profitable bottom line.

But competition in the auction space is fierce. Yahoo! and Amazon opened their own branded auction sites, along with literally hundreds of other lesser-known general auctions and thousands of specialized Web bidding sites. There is also a continuous stream of new dot-coms looking to profit from the online auction growth engine. eBay has tried to block product/price comparison tools from combing its site and pulling off lists of specific auction items that can then be compared with the bidding prices on other sites, but its defensiveness has garnered criticism. New businesses such as Andalé.com offer tools that make it easier for the most prolific auction sellers to manage accounts at a number of different auction sites simultaneously, threatening to loosen the dependence and the positive relationship that eBay has worked to create with its extremely valuable critical mass of "power sellers."

Recognizing that its millions of daily visitors are value sources in their own right, the company has struck a number of lucrative partnership deals that feature value-added services. Carclub.com, for example, a comprehensive portal for automotive information and services, entered into an agreement with eBay in the summer of 1999 to provide automotive-related services for eBay users. When individuals want to buy or sell a used car through eBay, carclub will provide an onsite inspection and warranty option that can add considerably to the car's value. eBay benefits by extending its mantle of trust to the typically risky person-to-person used car market, while carclub gets access to the entire eBay community in order to market its broader insurance and car warranty programs.

"The opportunity for online auto trading, although very significant, has been largely untapped," said carclub.com CEO Michael London in a press release covering the new partnership. "We expect that carclub.com's unique inspection process and other service offerings, combined with eBay's leadership in online person-to-person trading, will give us the ability to create the number one auto trading destination on the Internet."[3]

Another partnership leverages eBay's minute-to-minute information stream of bids on different auctions throughout the day. eBay has partnered with SkyTel to offer its users a line of eBay-branded pagers from SkyTel. In addition to all the standard pager functions, these will provide eBay members with regular updates on the progress of the auctions they are participating in, sending alerts at preset critical moments.

To expand its value system beyond the auction space and keep ahead of the competition, eBay has focused increased attention on providing different types of services for its current stream of buyers and sellers. It is also working to attract the millions of other Net users who have yet to be converted to the auction mode. To move up the quality ladder, eBay executives decided to buy Butterfield & Butterfield, a traditional bricks-and-mortar auction house that specializes in premium auctions of antiques, fine art, and collectibles from around the world. And despite a vow to maintain its focus on the consumer-to-consumer marketplace, eBay has also opened a small business exchange to obtain a share of the lucrative business-to-business purchasing transactions.

Conclusion

Amazon, Yahoo!, and eBay have each assembled some of the essential building blocks for a digital value system. But, as Jeff Bezos noted, success on the Internet is far from guaranteed—even with the right ingredients.

The digital value system framework encapsulates insights that still elude many companies, even those that cut their teeth on the Web. Instead of a chain of carefully connected and smoothly flowing activities, companies need to facilitate a wide variety of relationships of different duration (some very short, others long-standing) and varying degrees of closeness and trust. The key goal is to generate value for others—customers, vendors, partners, etc.—and to maximize the total value that is available to all participants instead of focusing on adding value exclusively to the central enterprise.

The future growth of all companies will be based on a closer alignment of company interests with a focus on the overall good for everyone in the marketplace—partners and customers. That is the ultimate pathway to maximum digital value. The companies that aim at attracting the most participants into their digital value systems and establish increasing returns for those participants will grow faster, stay more flexible, and become more profitable than companies that try to maximize individual returns. Making sure that everyone wins puts more value on the table for the next round and attracts even more players to join and add their own stakes. That is the wellspring of increasing digital returns.

Shifting from simply doing business on the Internet to launching a digital value system requires companies to reevaluate their overall strategy, the integration of network applications throughout the organization, and their relationships with supply and distribution channels, business partners, customers, and competitors. It's a formidable challenge, all the more so because maximum value involves balancing and coordinating all these factors dynamically and interactively rather than as separate areas of responsibility.

Smoothly functioning value systems are essential for dot-coms and traditional companies alike. The next five chapters will analyze in more detail how information, trust, relationships, services, and e-brokerage contribute individually and collectively to create new opportunities for digital value and provide a foundation for long-term success in the Internet economy.

C H A P T E R F O U R

Information
The Purest Form of Value

The premise that all enterprises are information businesses at their core has passed from strategic insight to common sense. Once companies engage in any form of e-commerce, however, managers face a host of new strategic questions about the relative value of information. The massive migration of digital data to the Web underscores the importance of information as a fundamental corporate asset, even as it raises more complex issues about access, ownership, and use. How much is the information that a company already possesses worth on the electronic marketplace? What investment should it make in protecting that which is known and acquiring that which is not? Which is more valuable to the individual corporation—obtaining access to scarce information and keeping it within a small inner circle as long as possible, or taking part in a free global information exchange by sharing information openly with all the parties who are willing to share in return?

These are not just idle debating points. Selling products and supporting customers on the Web require day-to-day decisions about information disclosure. Someone has to think about the broader consequences of placing global prices on the corporate Web site. Sharing

71

real-time inventory availability and forthcoming product announcements will certainly benefit some customers. On the other hand, revealing this information to competitors or to international customers may open the door to price wars and strain relationships with the firm's existing distribution channels. Hosting information about related products made by independent firms or even competitors' inventory and product information may help to establish market leadership or may simply siphon off orders. We will analyze these issues in the context of a strategy for turning information into value in the Internet economy.

The Limits of Information Hoarding

The stock management response tends to place a higher value on protecting proprietary information rather than sharing it. In fact, the practice of traditional corporations has been to keep much of their core strategic information strictly walled off from prying eyes. Even employees typically do not get to see the full extent of the data that is collected and stored up by the organization. In a competitive business climate, knowing more than the competition is seen as a source of advantage to be carefully guarded. Giving away information to friend and foe alike sounds like a losing strategy.

Classic information theory would seem to reinforce the position of hoarding scarce information to maximize its value to insiders. As part of his groundbreaking work on the impact of information discovery and sharing in the 1940s, Claude E. Shannon noted that the more certain the outcome of an experiment is in advance, the less information is gained from that outcome.[1]

The value of being in possession of new information—such as the outcome of an experiment or the latest data about how many units of a newly released product have sold this week on the company's Web site—would thus seem to depend at least in part on others being unable to access this information. This assumes an implicit "first-knower" advantage. The less that competitors and outsiders know, the more valuable the insider information can become. Indeed, withholding information from potential competitors and even sowing misinformation in the marketplace are well-worn competitive strategies.

In contrast, corporations that espouse a digital value model look at information sharing as a strategic asset. Michel Dell, for example, asserts, "The Internet makes it possible to bring customers and suppliers inside your business, to share openly critical business information and applications, to create true information partnerships. These partnerships, formed around information access, will transform traditional notions of economic value."[2]

The Internet undermines competitive strategy based on information scarcity by making every Web site into a potential channel for free distribution of anything and everything that can be transmitted digitally. Companies have to adjust to the fact that the Internet changes the nature and the value of information just as much as it changes the value of their own internal processes for information management. On the Internet, the saying goes, information wants to be free. Not just free in the sense of available without any significant cost to the end user, but free in its circulation around the globe to anyone who can access the Web and free to trigger decisions and coordinate action within a digital value system. In a situation where secrecy has become almost impossible, the rationale for protecting information is less compelling, and the pressure to turn information into value as quickly as possible has increased. As the following examples illustrate, the value of online information is realized only in action.

From Aggregation to Action

Ubiquitous Internet access for businesses and consumers alike turns traditional information theories inside out. As companies consider their Internet information strategy, the primary question is how to transform all available information into value for themselves and for their partners and customers. A core tenet of the Internet economy is that the value of information increases directly in proportion to the speed with which a company can act on the information.

Aggregation and rapid reuse of information are the most obvious activities of successful Internet ventures. Visits to Web sites generate insights into customer preferences, and profiles of customers generate personalized online offers while the customer is still connected. Internet community, infomediary, and portal models are all based on amassing information in real time and converting it almost instantaneously into action. The value of Internet-based companies is directly related to the velocity at which they are able to process all of the bits collected via the Web and turn them into some type of value generation—everything from that real-time discount on the Web to a custom-designed product or service, a well-placed advertisement, or an alliance with the provider for something that the bits indicate will soon be in demand.

The progression from information to action that releases the information's value is particularly visible in those Web enterprises that are grounded almost entirely in circulating information rather than tangible goods. Yahoo!'s valuation goes up when new users decide to register for personalized services, not just because of dollars that change hands, but because the information that those users bring will enrich the overall pool of demographic insight and personal detail. Yahoo! has demonstrated its ability to turn the information from millions of individual registrations and billions of click streams into specific, targeted partnerships, marketing messages, and personalized services. Without this finely tuned strategy for transforming the information about its users into action, the expense of supporting these millions of Web visitors would quickly outstrip their direct and even their potential revenue. This is one of the lessons from the demise of Pathfinder, discussed in chapter 3, and other early Web sites. Information is for action not accumulation.

Similarly, if eBay simply logged all the information about seller rankings and buyer transactions that took place on its site without having a way to turn this information into action, it would be spending resources without generating value. But by analyzing these ratings and publishing them on the Web, it turned them into a resource that served to generate buyer/seller trust and ignite mass bidding. A less

Web-centric model might have led to a system that tried to earn revenues from the rankings directly, publishing them offline or allowing them to be searched for a fee along the lines of Dun & Bradstreet. But making the maximum amount of information freely available to all turned out to be the catalyst that fueled a larger stream of overall auction revenues.

In the business-to-business realm, some of the greatest values that emerging online marketplaces offer to end users are their detailed catalogs, content, and product specification information. These resources enable customers to determine from a single online search whether a particular item matches their requirements and to order it immediately from the vendor offering the best terms. In the realm of scientific equipment or electronic components, for example, it was difficult and time-consuming for scientists and engineers who needed a specific product to search through dozens of paper catalogs from multiple vendors. All of this information was available from the vendors themselves in different formats, but that didn't solve the problem from the point of view of the user. Searching the individual company Web sites was an improvement over paper, but still not a one-stop solution. Users immediately saw the value generated by a Web site that successfully aggregated all the related products into a single, easy-to-search format. Even though all the information had already been available to the end user in different forms, vertical portals built a billion-dollar business by making existing product information more actionable.

Despite their massive investment in information infrastructure and aggregation, the world's largest corporations are at a disadvantage in dealing with the dynamic, interactive information environment of the Internet because they lack the tools to integrate and query their databases in real time. Ray Lane, Oracle's former president and chief operating officer, notes that traditional companies typically have the most difficulty with pinning down even the simplest pieces of information, such as the exact number of employees on the payroll at any given moment in time. Even though Oracle's own products are designed for the effective organization and retrieval of huge quantities of information, Lane admits that his company is not exempt from information fragmentation, lack of real-time access, and delayed decision making. Until 1999, for example, Oracle's senior managers typically received sales reports two weeks after they had been processed through many levels of the corporate structure and containing only old news at a time when immediate responsiveness was essential for survival. It required a major consolidation of dozens of disparate databases within Oracle for managers to begin receiving more timely reports.

According to Lane, Oracle and other Global 1000 companies will never keep up with the pace of change on the Net unless they address this information time lag. Internet firms, he notes, are not burdened with a welter of legacy systems and incompatible databases. The newest companies often have the greatest ability to put the information they collect to work immediately:

> Amazon.com knows from hour to hour what is being sold because all the information that is being generated by all of its servers is then fed into a single integrated application. That has incredible implications for decision making and competitiveness. Amazon can change direction, adjust its prices and products, even transform its business model based on current, consolidated information about its entire business performance while traditional companies are relying on forecasts, two-week old data, and guesswork.[3]

Most traditional companies have vast treasure troves of information about their customers already stored in their current systems, and they are busily collecting more data from the Internet. As the Oracle story illustrates, it is extremely difficult for large organizations, even technology companies, to integrate all this information and to access it in real time in ways that will turn it into value for themselves and for their customers. This may be because over the years system designers have worked very hard to homogenize customer information—to slice it, dice it, and run it down the aisles and through the checkout counters as quickly as possible. The goal was processing efficiency rather than added value and customization. Even when corporate managers actively seek to turn existing data into grist for new value creation in the real-time Internet environment, the odds are against success. The lack of standards in the way it has been collected—fragmented and dedicated to one application at a time—means that most legacy information tends to remain stuck in back-end systems that are difficult for even key people within the corporation to penetrate, let alone make accessible to the marketplace. Today's Web data collection practices tend only to contribute to these problems by piling up even more silos of rapidly accumulating data about visitors, profiles, and online traffic patterns without generating any decision-oriented insights about individual customer interests and needs.

Distribution of business processes among a number of online partners and the shifting role of customers and suppliers make improved management of all information a priority. But most companies—whether rooted in bricks and mortar or centered on the Internet—still squander the information they collect through the Net. This is not because they don't understand that it represents a valuable asset in the global electronic marketplace but because they don't know how to get the value out—how to unchain the value. They are locked in a mind-set that says value is dependent on only their knowing the information. In the fluid marketplace of the Web, information value is realized only through sharing, not through hoarding.

To see beyond the immediate impact of information strategy for any single company, it is essential to have a framework that can apply equally well to large, technology-oriented organizations, traditional corporations, and the most recently formed dot-com enterprises. The central question for all of these players is what information structures are most likely to generate action by the largest number of participants, thus releasing the greatest amount of value. In order to address this question and to understand how the answer has changed over the past several years of online activity, we will describe three increasingly expansive stages of information sharing between and among organizations and between companies and their customers in an Internet-enabled marketplace. This chapter provides an analysis of B2B information sharing as a catalyst for digital value. Chapter 5 discusses how the information dynamic shifts in a business-to-consumer (B2C) environment.

Three Degrees of Information Sharing

Information sharing across all corporations, from the most restrictive type of dissemination to the most open, consists of three distinct forms of interchange, namely, information exchange, information access, and information pooling. Each of these plays an important role in business-to-business interactions but, as we shall see, makes very different contributions to the distillation of information and its conversion into action.

Information Exchange

Information exchange, the first degree of information sharing among corporations, deals in the minimal amount of information needed to conduct business at all and typically stays within the boundaries of what is required to take the next step in the desired transaction. Information exchange includes, for example, the transmission of specifications, order quantities, desired delivery times, and data attendant to the negotiation of price.

At the information exchange level of information sharing each firm typically sends and receives only what is required to consummate a specific deal with another member of the value chain. A defining characteristic of information exchange is that it is "pair-wise." That is to say, the information is specific to the business at hand and is not generally available in the same way at the same time to all business partners. When Acme quotes a price for widgets to Beacon on Wednesday for delivery on Friday, only Acme and Beacon know the details of this quote. The price and delivery schedule that Acme quotes to Capital on Thursday is not necessarily the same and in the pair-wise mode Acme ensures that Capital has no way of finding out about the offer just made to Beacon.

The information exchange process is easily captured by forms and templates because it is highly formalized and repetitive. Much of the data exchanged between companies at this level is simply details about a specific transaction that is covered by standing agreements and contracts. Acme and Beacon have already established the widget specifications and the general purchase terms. The only new information concerns availability, spot purchase price, and delivery schedule. This type of information has become the grist for electronic data interchange (EDI) because it requires almost no human judgment and can be managed by computers on either side of the exchange.

Even though it is routine and limited in many ways, information exchange yields value and in fact provides a hint as to why information sharing in general gives more than it takes. If companies were unwilling to quote prices or commit to delivery dates to anybody else, there would not be much of a marketplace. Firms have to share information to conduct business, and the predictability of this routine exchange lends itself to the type of efficiencies that can be harvested by EDI systems.

Making even the most routine information exchange as efficient as possible yields a secondary value. It reduces the bureaucratic friction in the business processes between two firms. This efficiency is created not by the information itself but rather by the trust that it comes wrapped in. What makes EDI work isn't the computer programs shared between the firms but the contract that they sign before the first bit travels down the wire. The contract creates the trust, which in turn makes the bits instantly and unhesitatingly actionable. In our example, Beacon has established a prior agreement with Acme about the size and performance of the widgets and will proceed to pay the agreed-on price for this shipment based on that existing contract. As chapter 5 will discuss in more detail, trust is an information catalyst. It accelerates the process of turning the information into action. Lack of trust on the other hand is an action inhibitor. If information is not reinforced with trust in some form or another, then it will not be acted on for fear that the actions would prove to be wrong seen in the light of the correct information. If Beacon has to measure all the widgets before authorizing payment, that would certainly reduce the value of the information that the shipment had arrived.

Information exchange typically does not alter the relationship of the two organizations involved in the exchange nor change their place in the value chain. No reading is provided as to whether or not what one is selling or buying should be changed in any meaningful way. At this level, firms do not get to see very far into each other's business and are not motivated to consider how shifts in one company's internal processes might be of mutual value. All the firms see is essentially quantity ordered and price paid, and thus these are the only two variables that can be manipulated. How many do you want and what are you willing to pay? A firm can get better and better at what it does, but it receives few signals to do something different. The value chain and the role of each firm in it tends to remain stable, as does the relationship of each firm to the others as long as there are no significant changes in the external environment.

Information exchange leads to relationship optimization and the continuous improvement of the accuracy and efficiency of communications between each pair of companies. The relationship of each of the firms to each other is constantly adjusted so that that particular relationship—in isolation from all the other relationships—runs at peak efficiency. If this is the case, increasing the efficiency in one relationship may simultaneously decrease the efficiency in another, so if one does reach a steady state, it is one of uniformly distributed inefficiency rather than a marketwide minimum of inefficiency.

Information Access

At the second stage of information sharing, information access, the relationship between two firms engaging in business changes dramatically. Information access is characteristic of the strategy used by Dell, Ford, and other companies that have opened up their supply chains to outside participants. Once firms allow their suppliers and their customers to access internal operational databases, they are opening the door to a much more advanced level of partnership with these entities. Not only is information directly relating to a firm's external relationships to other firms exposed, but the information behind the decisions driving those relationships may also be available or easily inferred. Engineering drawings, product plans, market forecasts, and projected needs and requirements are all pasted on the side of the barn for all participants to see. Of course, the process of information access can itself unfold in different stages and levels of disclosure. Perhaps the firm will start by simply letting a limited number of preferred suppliers have access to the relevant inventory information and production schedules in the corporate intranet. Ford, for example, expanded and streamlined its just-in-time supplier relationships by opening its intranet to the suppliers of key auto and truck components and letting those suppliers organize direct, as-needed delivery to the appropriate assembly plants. At a more advanced stage of information access, firms open themselves to full access, with the attendant openness to changing direction at the request of partners for the mutual benefit of all.

Dell has made the practice of shared information access into a finely tuned strategy for cost savings and efficiency in inventory and production management. By shifting the responsibility for inventory management and component assembly to its suppliers and partners, Dell has redefined the business model for the entire industry. This new model puts the squeeze on distribution channels and on manufacturers such as Compaq that have not been as aggressive in implementing shared information strategies. One frequently discussed benefit of this system is that Dell saves both time and money by moving responsibility to its suppliers in exchange for open access to information. Even more important in terms of shaping Dell's overall direction is the insight that mutual information access provides to Dell's management.

It is important to note that Dell does not limit itself to a one-sided type of information sharing, where the suppliers and customers see only the orders required for the specific assembly and shipment of a particular computer. This would be an actionable window into Dell, but it would not challenge Dell to rethink its internal decisions. Instead, customers are also allowed insider access to Dell's future product and development plans and are encouraged to share the same with Dell to better synchronize and meet each other's needs. Dell has dubbed this process "direct commerce integration" and notes on its

Web site, "More than 30,000 companies now have customer pages on Dell's site, which include not only configurations their IT departments have approved, but also future product road maps, pricing guidelines, and just about any other piece of information that is relevant to a transaction."[4]

With direct commerce integration, all the parties that access information through Dell recognize a mutual value in coordinating and occasionally changing development directions. As their business needs change, participants have a place to make that known to Dell. One or two corporate customer shifts might not be enough to stimulate the computer company to respond with any major rethinking of its own development plans, but if hundreds or thousands of corporate customers start to register a particular need, the company will be in an ideal position to turn this insight into action much more quickly than its competitors.

Unlike information exchange, information access tends to equalize the information holdings of all of a firm's trading partners. Clearly there is an efficiency gain to the firm because now it just maintains one database and one access channel, whereas in information exchange, it had to manage the data for and the channel to each trading partner. But this IT savings is secondary to the real value of information access. An open access database says to the marketplace, "These are the facts, and these are my decisions. Conduct yourself accordingly." This invites the firm's trading partners to provide additional facts or to offer alternative analyses of the existing facts in order to affect those decisions. In effect, it invites these marketplace partners to share in the decision-making process and to actually improve the firm's factual foundation and thus to improve the firm itself.

Information access does bring some risks along with its benefits. Dell's plans and product line information are much more exposed to scrutiny and competitive response. But the value to Dell of opening up its internal processes to the marketplace is immense. It has allowed the company to totally rethink the process of computer manufacture and distribution and has given it a window into the development and technology plans of thousands of its largest and most important customers. As long as Dell is able to turn these insights into timely action, it will stay ahead of its competition because, even when they look at identical information, they will not be in a position to pull ahead. In a very real way, Dell's continuous information access has primed the company to be ready for constant action, and this effect is much harder to replicate than the information itself.

Whereas information exchange leads only to a limited benefit for each participant in the form of pair-wise relationship optimization, information access leads to firm optimization. The segmentation of the overall market remains fixed, but the information necessary for a firm to reconsider its role within that segmentation is now available. By gaining visibility into its trading partner's processes, a firm can make suggestions to better synchronize those processes with its own, yielding enhanced value for both. Partners can actually change the relationship between themselves rather than just tune a fixed relationship, and they can use these changes to establish a sustainable lead in the critical processes for their product.

Information Pooling

The third and, for the purposes of our discussion, most extensive form of information sharing is information pooling. At this stage, all firms in the value system contribute to and access a common database. Governmental statistics and industrial standards are obvious examples of information sharing through pooling. In the Internet context, information pooling is best exemplified by the rapid rise of infomediaries and Web portals that are focused on a particular industry. There are now thousands of such specialized vertical portals, or vortals, covering all the major industry sectors along with every imaginable product family, from cow embryos to molded plastic components and from batteries to blood plasma.

The primary objective and advantage of information pooling is cooperative action: competing firms work together to take inefficiencies, which benefit no one, out of the marketplace. The recent spate of industry consortia set up to deal with online standards and technology development is another prime example of information pooling. Consortia are creations of the information age. Common information wants to be converted into cooperative action, and traditional standards bodies were simply too slow in making this transformation. In fact, this is the quantum change in information handling that the Internet has wrought: it's not what you know; it's how fast you use it. Information does not deliver anything near its potential value until it has stimulated action.

With information pooling in place, not only do all firms in a digital value system see the same data, they cooperate in altering the values of the data. The reality represented by the data becomes the common platform—the given wisdom, the weltanschauung—that is assumed by the firms and hence all the customers of the market. Information pooling, therefore, leads to market optimization, and this may, in fact, mean market resegmentation. In effect, the firms in the market form an information-driven *keiretsu*. Raw, nose-to-nose competition declines, individual roles are assumed, and effort is spent on efficiently delivering a product with a minimum of intramarket friction and competition.

Figure 4-1 illustrates the progression we have described in terms of the amount of shared information and the degree of market efficiency achieved. As more companies join the Internet economy, the incentives to work toward efficient markets are on the rise.

Given the characterization of information sharing and the description of the value created at each plateau, as shown in figure 4-1, it becomes easier to discern the increasing value that is generated by information on the Internet. As we move from information exchange to access to pooling, two new kinds of information are brought into being. First, all market participants start to see global implications of the information rather than just local impact. This means they have a more complete and more accurate picture of the state of the overall market. Second, the position of the firms in relation to each other is revealed. X knows what Y knows, and Y knows what X knows, and X knows what Y knows about what X knows, etc. What X knows is part of the global state of the market, but it is meta-state. We can separate

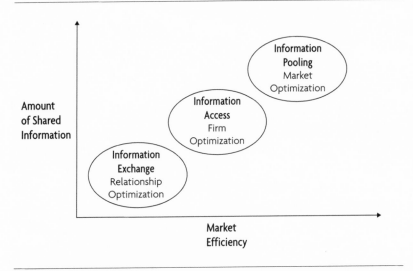

Figure 4-1 Stages of Information Sharing

this information and its potential value from simply knowing the basic facts of how many widgets X sold.

The effectiveness of a market as seen by the customer is, however, not directly dependent on simply the amount of information that circulates within it. If none of the firms change their behavior based on different levels of information, then the information has no effect on the market. Changing the amount of information in the market or the distribution of information through the market does not of itself lead to a cycle of increasing value. What the customer cares about is the change—the responsiveness—of the market under various conditions. In the case at hand, the customer cares about the responsiveness of the market with respect to various degrees of information sharing. How do the three information sharing regimens perform on this benchmark? Table 4-1 ranks information exchange, information access, and information pooling in terms of the amount of information available and the incentive for action that it provides.

In the information exchange regimen, information concealment is part and parcel of the overall culture of the market. Firms don't take

	AMOUNT OF INFORMATION	INCENTIVE TO ACT
Information Exchange	Too Little	None
Information Access	Too Much	Some
Information Pooling	Just the Right Amount	Mandatory

Table 4-1 Impact of Information-Sharing Levels on Action Levels

very big chances because there simply is very little information on which to base change of any sort and there is no incentive to change. In fact there is every incentive not to change. A firm orders what it needs, gets the best price it can, produces for its customers, and goes back to the beginning. Even though there may be free-radical value in the interstices of the market, firms will never cash in on it because they can't find it.

In the information access regimen, information is plentiful, but there is only a weak call to action. Firms can see what other companies are doing and make suggestions for coordinated change, but they can just as easily simply engage in self-tuning and adjust their own behavior to optimize on a day-to-day basis.

In the information pooling regimen, firms have both the information and the incentive to act. Indeed each firm must act because action is the only basis of competitive edge. The market, just like a stock market, is driven by participants' taking advantage of information. In other words, the market becomes more and more like an open auction. Companies that are still at the stage of basic information exchange will be hard pressed to keep up with these developments.

Managing Information Sharing

Will all firms inevitably move from the less-flexible and less-value-enhancing forms of information sharing to the more-comprehensive information pooling? Ironically, even though the Internet provides a very strong push in this direction, it also offers the alternative approach of operating a trio of information outlets—the public Web site, the extranet, and the intranet—and calibrating the degree of openness much more narrowly to the functions at hand. That brings us back to the opening question of this chapter: How do companies determine when it is to their advantage to share information openly and when it is still in their best interests to keep details of pricing, product specifications, and customer relations under wraps, or at least confined to a limited-access extranet?

The model of a digital value system operating within an open market context and the insight that information sharing increases a firm's ability to obtain value from information provide a systematic way to address this question. Within any digital value system, open information access among leading companies, partners, suppliers, and customers will increase the ability of all participants to act on the information, thereby generating a cycle of actions leading to expanding value. Dell Computers provides an example of an information-based system in practice.

Internet infomediaries and vertical portals are attempting to motivate information pooling in industries where digital value systems are less prevalent or have not reached critical mass in terms of supplier and buyer participation. Large companies that overlap with online infomediaries often try to hold the line on information sharing by refusing to list their products and prices on the infomediary Web site. But unless they are prepared to enlarge their own online programs to include all the information needed to trigger customer action (typically including competitive product listings), they will not be able to hold out against the greater value of shared information over the long term. Customers want to see the market as a whole, not collect bits of market information by visiting individual Web sites. Therefore, a critical mass of customers will inevitably gravitate to the provider of the most valuable and actionable information, and no one company can compete with this trend. Companies whose data is not in the pool are out of the shopper's sight and out of the shopper's mind.

A close look at the role of information in the digital value system affirms that the optimal value for all parties comes from an information-pooling model. So the real decision is whether a particular company is better off attempting to create its own information-sharing system, and motivating competitors and potential customers to participate, or better off joining one or more existing vertical portals. If your firm is considering creating its own system, you should ask the following basic questions:

- What is your current market share? Market leaders that can draw on established relationships with complementary product providers and suppliers have the best opportunity for establishing critical mass in a new e-marketplace.

- Can you fully integrate product, inventory, and delivery information in real time to create an information pool that will be accessible to all of the value system partners and customers?

- What is your level of flexibility and competitiveness on pricing?

- How quickly can you analyze and act on the flow of information that is generated by the system?

The ability to transform information into action more quickly than the competition is the key advantage of information pooling, as we have seen.

Companies that decide to participate in an existing portal need to address whether they would be getting the same or greater information flow from the portal as from their own Web efforts. If the flow is not adequate, they risk being cut off from vital customer and supplier insights and actionable information. It is essential to maintain direct access to the following types of data:

- how customers are viewing your information (gathered from reports and analysis about customer search and navigational behavior on the site);

- how your company compares with the rest of the portal participants in attracting traffic and converting visits to orders;

- key points of preference and decisions made on the part of customers behind the purchase process across the entire portal (gleaned from what types of searches are undertaken; how many comparisons are made; and how factors driving purchases, such as price versus availability, influence decisions); and

- overview of the aggregate customer information for the entire portal (size of average purchase and information about the types of companies that are regular participants).

The logic of information pooling also dictates that specialized vertical marketplaces will themselves begin to aggregate into meta-markets that span several interrelated industries. We will return to this development in chapter 8 with a more detailed discussion of the brokered economy.

Information Pooling as a Business Model

We have seen that information pooling provides benefits to existing companies that participate in open information systems and to their customers. The information-pooling model has also generated a number of new Internet ventures that aim at capturing some of this value for themselves, most notably those that are aggregating information and suppliers to facilitate industry-wide online purchasing systems. The implications of information pooling for e-marketplaces and dynamic pricing will be discussed in more detail in chapter 8. The analysis of business-to-business examples that follows demonstrates the range of opportunities created by pooling online information— from operating a comprehensive scientific equipment portal to creating value around free, open source software to establishing a virtual publishing and distribution system for business information.

SciQuest

SciQuest, an Internet venture based in Raleigh, North Carolina, offers a vertical information portal specializing in facilitating the online purchase of scientific supplies and equipment. Success in this competitive space requires placing a premium on quality and depth of information, so SciQuest has built its value proposition on having the best-organized and most-comprehensive product information. Goal number one was developing a Web site that would attract scientists and other end users of the equipment. The premise was that drawing a critical mass of these users regularly to the SciQuest Web site would create the incentive for suppliers and advertisers to participate. According to founder and former VP of business development, Payton Anderson, perfecting the product information available to buyers is good for the marketplace as a whole and especially good for his company in the long run. Comprehensive information draws the scientists and the laboratory end users to the SciQuest portal in large numbers, but the value system is not complete without vendors who are willing to sell their products through the Web site.

The SciQuest experience in convincing vendors to take part in their portal is typical of many Internet exchanges. The perceived value of participation varies with the size and market dominance of the vendor. In particular, smaller vendors come to see value in the partnership faster than the dominant market brands. It is a challenge to convince large vendors that selling through a portal benefits them, especially when it puts their products and prices side by side with those of competitors. What is good for the consumer and the marketplace as a whole does not necessarily reflect the self-interest of market leaders. However, SciQuest's focus on providing high-value information in order to bring hundreds of thousands of scientists into its value orbit has been a key factor in bringing the largest vendors into the portal, as Anderson states:

> Customer demand is an essential driver for our business. The more we do to make finding and buying the right equipment easier, the more they put

pressure on vendors who aren't part of SciQuest yet. Suppliers are starting to realize that the customers want them to participate one way or another and that we can work with them to generate value in the process. It's true that weak suppliers will be exposed as being weak but that may force them to change. Those that can compete effectively will win more business in the long run.[5]

Founded in 1995, SciQuest was an early player in online information pooling. Now they are part of a crowd. The past few years have seen a wave of consolidation among the company's competitors, even as the number of vertical portals across all industries has mushroomed from a few dozen to over a thousand. More consolidation is likely, since portals need to deliver a critical mass of buyers and transactions to generate revenues. As Anderson notes, high quality information, and lots of it, is an essential magnet for buyers. But this is not enough. SciQuest must also deepen its relationships with vendors and help them to turn the information generated through its portal into more effective action. Transforming itself from portal to digital value system is the best way for SciQuest to differentiate itself from new competitors and create loyal vendors as well as buyers.

Putting yourself at the center of your own value network means figuring out how to create increasing digital returns for your key customers and strategic partners so that they will return over and over again instead of being attracted by a better offer. It means ensuring that your products and services get better (as defined by your customers and your noncustomers) in advance of market expectations and customer demand. It means that you are smarter, faster, and more flexible on your feet and that your partners continually get smarter, faster, and more profitable because they are working with you. One strategy for accomplishing this feat is to put the community to work in making your product better and better all the time.

This is the philosophy behind the open source software movement. Software developers around the world voluntarily work on open source systems to add features and eliminate bugs. Every new improvement is distributed over the Internet and freely available for others to use. The result is robust code that has been thoroughly tested by some of the best minds in the industry. It is a great model for continual improvement, but a difficult challenge in terms of creating revenues. Why would anyone pay a company for a product that they could obtain for free from multiple locations on the Net? That's the challenge that Red Hat has taken on in building a value system based on the open source Linux operating system.

Red Hat

Since its debut in 1994, Red Hat, a Linux software company based in Durham, North Carolina, has been crafting a business case for information sharing in the software industry. Its branded version of the open source Linux operating system is one of the most popular and most recognized names among dedicated Linux users, but Red Hat executives are the first to admit that Linux itself is hardly a household name. As an alternative to Microsoft's dominant computer operating systems, it is clearly playing the role of David against a still-powerful Goliath. But gaining brand recognition is only one of the challenges facing a company that is attempting to build a business model around an open source product.

Since many versions of Linux are available for free, generating growth and revenues around Red Hat Linux was a formidable challenge. The company's strategy was to build an Internet-based digital value framework from the ground up. By providing discussion groups and a Web site focused on online support for Linux developers, along with access to the latest software releases, Red Hat established its reputation as a center for Linux development. As the size of the developer community grew and the number of regular visitors to Red Hat's Web site soared, potential partners and advertisers began to take note. In 1998, Dell announced that Red Hat software would be available as a factory installation option on selected workstations and desktop PCs, a major boost for Red Hat's market penetration. Subscription-based support services and software upgrade licenses began to take shape as solid revenue streams. Bolstered by an extremely loyal community of Linux users, Red Hat established itself as a leading provider of "industrial strength" versions of the Linux system. Larger customers that were interested in the stability and extensibility of the system but didn't want to deal with in-house support were attracted to the Red Hat license and support agreements, and the company's revenue from support contracts more than tripled in 1999.

This rapid growth, loyal partners and users, and a business built on value added services has powered Red Hat to the top of the open source providers. To consolidate its lead among the development community, Red Hat acquired another leading Linux developer, Cygnus Solutions, in the fall of 1999 and announced a strategic alliance with Dell to factory-install Red Hat on Dell's line of servers, as well as to provide subsidized Red Hat support and installation services for Dell's server customers.

According to Manoj George, former Red Hat CFO, the strategy of turning information into action in terms of constantly improving the software products is really working for Red Hat:

> Our goal is not to put up barriers but to execute well and fast and consistently, so we don't worry about the traditional proprietary view of competition that is based on protecting information and guarding

intellectual property. The whole open source model is based on taking all the best parts that are developed by the community and putting them together in the best possible package. If someone else comes out with a better product based on Linux, that means the customer benefits, and we have our work cut out for us. Our company response has to be action. We can learn from that innovation, and now we'll have to do even better and quickly come up with the next development that customers will want.[6]

Like SciQuest, Red Hat is facing a number of new competitors as interest in Linux becomes more widespread. The company must execute on its goal of creating the best product from pooling the contributions of a worldwide developer community in order to maintain its lead.

Fatbrain.com

The evolution of Fatbrain.com demonstrates that even online firms must constantly reinvent themselves and extend their core offerings based on creatively mining and pooling information. Fatbrain.com started its existence in cofounder Chris MacAskill's Silicon Valley garage in 1995 with the more prosaic name of CBooks Express and the modest mission of selling computer books online. The fact that a little start-up in Seattle called Amazon was revving up its marketing engine about the same time at first seemed like a good omen for overall consumer acceptance of online book buying. But Amazon and a raft of online shops focusing on computer and Internet publications quickly became too much of a good thing, and CBooks had to struggle just to differentiate itself. After two years of solid but unspectacular growth, it was clear that

CBooks could not keep pace with its Internet-based rivals. CEO MacAskill took a hard look at the online competition in 1997 and decided that one source of differentiation might come from actually owning a bricks-and-mortar bookstore with a significant in-house inventory available for same-day shipping. The acquisition of Computer Literacy Books proved to be another short-term advance, however, soon trumped by Amazon's more aggressive move to acquire one of the leading book wholesalers. Even though the Computer Literacy bookstores were profitable, they were not a stepping-stone to the increasing information value that MacAskill still hoped to create with his venture.

In 1999 Computer Literacy embarked on a transformation of its business model with an attention-grabbing new name— Fatbrain.com—and a new venture that focused directly on digital information. It launched eMatter, billed as "the invention of secure digital publishing for the masses." Using Fatbrain's own digital rights protection technology and hosted on the company's Web site, eMatter aims to become a new online information mecca for writers, publishers, and professionals. MacAskill notes that the eMatter platform brings Fatbrain's information value model full circle:

> Now our customers can become information publishers in their own right by putting their work up for sale on eMatter. Fatbrain generates new information and also gathers insight into how our content is being used and what topics are most in demand. We are facilitating information transfer in an industry where information is at the center of everything.[7]

These companies illustrate three models for turning information into action in a digital economy—aggregation of buyers and sellers, value-added services, and digital distribution. As more and more companies embrace these models and incorporate the other elements of digital value into their business models, early movers like SciQuest, Red Hat, and FatBrain are in danger of losing their advantage.

Conclusion

Information pooling provides an efficient and strategic way for online companies to move quickly and increase their responsiveness to the individual customer and the overall marketplace. It is important to note that the efficacy of information pooling in the business-to-business world is based on the assumption that each company retains control over its core information and exercises a conscious choice about the time and manner of its release. In fact, some companies have taken strong action against employees who have revealed information about a company to a third-party Web site or chat group without authorization, even when the employee did not claim to be representing the official company position. This type of individual and ad hoc disclosure of information doesn't fit into the information-pooling framework.

It is also clear that if a firm is to act quickly on information, then it must trust that information or more properly must trust the provider of the information. This is just as true if the provider is another firm in the marketplace as it is if the provider is the customer. If the information is incorrect, then actions will be counterproductive, and value will be destroyed. If value is lost, then trust will be eroded. Thus, this is a two-way street. The firm trusts the provider of the information and acts on it quickly without independent verification. The provider—the customer or business partner—trusts the firm to use the information to the provider's benefit.

The provider's trust in the firm leads to the provision of higher-quality information. The firm's trust in the provider leads to rapid action based on this information. The action leads to greater value for both the provider and the firm, reinforcing the trust each had in the other. Trust yields information, which in turn yields more value, which reinforces and increases the trust. Trust and information pooling are natural and complementary components of the business-to-business online marketplace.

It is tempting to take this model for obtaining more value from online information in the business-to-business world and apply it wholesale to the vast amount of consumer information that is collected directly and indirectly via the Web. But there are some critical differences between these two relationships. The issue of establishing online trust is more complex in the business-to-consumer world, and, as chapter 5 discusses, lack of consumer trust is a serious barrier to increasing digital returns.

CHAPTER   FIVE

The Dynamics of Digital Trust

If information is the engine of the Internet, then trust provides the essential oil for its friction-free operation. Despite the explosion of e-commerce transactions over the past several years, that oil is still in short supply, especially among consumers. Unlike the business-to-business world where trust-based electronic information exchange was well established even before the growth of the Net, the individual Internet user is typically a newcomer to the world of digital interaction. Trust, in the broadest sense, involves reliance on another party to do the right thing, now and in the future. The less one knows about that other party, the higher the level of trust must be to consummate a transaction—and the Internet is packed with unfamiliar names and unknown places. "Whom should I trust?" becomes a question of paramount importance when the individual consumer is confronted with millions of choices on the Web.

There are several attributes of the Internet that make establishing trust between consumers and online enterprises a particular challenge. First, the Internet does not provide those tangible touchstones of trust that consumers rely on instinctively in face-to-face or mail order catalog interactions. There is no way to look a merchant in the eye or to assess the physical condition of the storefront when dealing with a company on the Web. Even the printed catalogs that arrive month after month at the consumer's doorstep provide more of a sense of stability than a collection of images on a computer screen. Regional and geographic cues are disappearing as the Internet expands internationally. At the same time, the stakes get higher as larger purchases and more valuable transactions move to the Internet.

Not only is it difficult to establish online trust without the familiar cues of the physical world, but the Internet actually demands greater trust than face-to-face, telephone, or mail order purchases. In the bricks-and-mortar context, an individual is likely to have a number of unique and delimited trust relationships—with merchants on Main Street, with professional service providers, with financial institutions, and so on. Building such relationships is time-consuming and depends critically on person-to-person contact and interaction. But these interactions do not typically cause a lot of anxiety about unwanted information pooling. Consumers fill out health history forms at the dentist's office and hand over tax forms to accountants without any second thoughts about the information being aggregated. It even seems appropriate that our favorite airline keeps a file on our travel and diet preferences and that our health club knows all about our weight and fitness aspirations. Consumers rely on the physical and organizational boundaries that separate these different bricks-and-mortar businesses to create information-sharing barriers. In the past, the physical separation of these realms and the difficulties of moving data between different computer systems did indeed carry some built-in assurance that separate information-collecting arenas would remain separate.

In contrast, the Internet's lack of boundaries means that online information sharing has no inherent limitations whatsoever. Consumers have come to understand that having everything connected to everything else on the Web has a downside when it comes to protecting confidentiality and personal information. The personal profile form that someone fills out at online merchant A's Web site may be shared instantly with thousands of other Web merchants who are quite outside the control of the individual consumer. If merchant A takes part in several Web profiling and data-pooling programs, the information collected on its Web site is automatically forwarded to many other merchants. That data may eventually be linked to a more extensive personal profile that was filled out months ago at site C and possibly combined with demographic and financial information that is stored at site X. Some or all of these Web sites may also be keeping track of every single move that the consumer makes while visiting—logging every keystroke and decision into a massive personal preference analysis.

This process all takes place behind the scenes and may well generate a much deeper and more complete picture of an individual's Web browsing history and buying habits than that consumer ever intended to share with merchant A, never mind with all these unknown merchants down the line. Many consumers have only a dim sense that these online profiling and data linking processes exist on the Net and even less understanding of the technical details of how they work and how much of the shared data can be traced back to them as individuals. But the interconnectedness of the Net is enough to make them uneasy about how much information they are inadvertently leaking to any given Web site and who gets to look at it.

Finally, there is no obvious entity on the Internet to take responsibility for defending the consumer against misuse of personal information or even for defining what constitutes such misuse in the online environment. Decades of credit card use have made individuals familiar with the limits of their financial liability if their credit card is stolen or inaccurate charges are added to their bill. At worst, a quick call to the card association will stop any future charges, and they will be $50 out of pocket. But there is no parallel set of standard procedures for individuals worried that a Web site is passing around inaccurate or potentially damaging information about them. In the United States, at least, there seem to be no consistent rules that govern the conduct of Web sites' information-handling practices or any clear recourse for individuals when things go wrong.[1]

These unique Internet characteristics, and the reactions that consumers have to them, mean that digital trust is much harder to establish and harder to maintain than bricks-and-mortar trust. The Catch-22 for online companies is that many business models rely on access to personal data. But the more consumers understand how easily such data is collected about them on the Web the more suspicious they become, even though they have no explicit evidence that any particular Web site will mistreat their information. Given these circumstances, it is not surprising that consumers are concerned about placing their trust in online merchants. But no matter how difficult it is to earn digital trust, every online company is vitally dependent on it to be successful on the Internet. It is essential, therefore, for managers to understand the critical difference between digital trust and bricks-and-mortar trust in order for them to send the right messages to their customers starting with the first encounter.

Overcoming barriers to online trust is a particularly urgent priority for newly emerging online brands that don't have any track record or physical presence in the bricks-and-mortar world. In fact, this is an area where traditional companies have a significant initial advantage in being able to move existing customer relationships onto the Web and to leverage the recognition of their established brands. That makes mastering the dynamics of digital trust the number one agenda item for new Internet companies. If they don't get consumers over the trust barrier, it will be impossible to turn the potential value of online visits into any real, sustainable advantage or customer loyalty. Without an understanding of how to build strong foundations of trust, business-to-consumer dot-coms are heading for failure.

This chapter outlines a digital trust hierarchy to illustrate the stages of online trust in business-to-consumer interactions and then analyzes some of the hazards of companies trying to short-circuit this process by collecting personal data without first obtaining consumer buy-in. It ends with a discussion of the consumer privacy backlash against current online merchant practices and a positive approach to creating shared value through information exchange and pooling in the consumer realm.

Differentiating between
Security and Digital Trust

It is important to distinguish at the outset between establishing wide-spectrum digital trust based on mutual sharing of information between consumer and online enterprise and simply providing a platform for secure online transactions. Most online companies are diligent about addressing Internet security issues, because they recognize that this protects their own interests as well as their customers. Managers cannot, however, assume that providing a technically secure Web site will guarantee a high level of consumer trust. There is no question that security is an essential component of electronic commerce. Every Internet user wants assurance that sensitive information such as credit card data is not subject to hijacking by malicious outsiders. But consumers are looking for more than protection from hackers when they think about trusting an online merchant. In fact, individual users today express at least as much concern about Web sites passing around their personal information as they do about transmission and possible theft of credit card numbers. An AT&T study of regular Internet users found that more than 80 percent had serious concerns about Web sites collecting data about them and using it in ways that they could not control.[2]

One reason for this concern is that the typical consumer's use of the Internet does not start out with the same assumptions and common interests as the business-to-business interactions we discussed in chapter 4. As online marketplaces become the norm for business trading, companies are recognizing that information pooling benefits all participants by enabling decisive action and eliminating unproductive steps in the fulfillment process. The acceleration of business processes that is driven by the Internet provides a strong argument in favor of information pooling as the catalyst to action for online enterprises. The value of business-to-business information pooling includes both the cost-savings due to more efficient commercial transactions and the longer-term value of creating a more market-responsive and adaptive business. Everyone has a chance to benefit from this type of information pooling.

If trust is a shared and community-reinforced value for online business-to-business activities, why aren't the same drivers of mutual trust at
work in the business-to-consumer world? Certainly parallels can be
drawn between the beneficial "pair-wise" exchange of information
between business-to-business participants and the activities between
an individual consumer and stand-alone Web site. In theory, the more
that individuals are willing to share information about interests, personal background, and their purchase preferences, the more effectively
online merchants can tailor offers to match these preferences, and the
more customized services the individual can choose from. Allowing
this information to be pooled among a group of merchants multiplies
the likelihood of an individual consumer receiving highly customized
services and special discount offers from the Web. But the rational progression from information exchange to information access to information pooling that we have seen in the business-to-business world does
not yet have a parallel in the business-to-consumer online environment.

Instead, the progression seems to lurch from online consumer
hesitation to behind the scenes information surveillance to company
collusion and eventually to consumer backlash. It's not a pretty picture. The logical model for the generation of mutually rewarding
trust in the business-to-business context obviously hits the rocks
when applied to consumer behavior on the Web. In a word, consumers don't buy it. Instead of starting from a premise that full disclosure is mutually beneficial, the average consumer needs to be convinced to trust anyone on the Internet. But instead of reassurance that
trust will be rewarded and respected, hesitant consumers are too often
left with an uneasy feeling that information is being extracted from
their online activities without their consent and that no tangible
rewards are forthcoming.

For starters, consumers tend to see much more clearly than merchants a distinction between providing security (a precondition for
engaging in transactions) and earning trust (an outcome of repeated
interactions and positive results over time). In the consumer's view,
the bricks-and-mortar parallel to Web site security is the uniformed
guard standing in the bank lobby. That guard serves an important
function, but he does not automatically qualify the bank for the type

of information sharing that takes place with a professional financial advisor or other trusted confidant. As bank customers, we may be pleased to see that the security guard is on duty, but we don't particularly want to share any details with him or the bank about our health status or our weekend plans. That information is reserved for our physician and our personal friends.

Online enterprises, however, often assert the prerogatives of trusted friends when they are only providing the services of security guards. What's worse, they seem unwilling to follow even the basic norms for earning trust in the physical world. First, they are nosy, with an annoying habit of eavesdropping on everything that we do online. Then they are gossips, eager to pass on tidbits behind our backs about our tastes in music or our buying habits to other Web sites we have never even met. It should be no surprise that consumers find such behavior untrustworthy and that learning about it after the fact often creates a backlash of ill will.

On the other hand, online companies have legitimate reasons for collecting, analyzing, and sometimes even sharing customer information with business partners. This data will make marketing messages and special offers more appealing and may be the foundation for valuable personalized services. How are companies to get the access they need to online information without risking the goodwill and future trust of their customers in the process?

The Digital Trust Hierarchy

Despite the importance of digital trust in establishing customer relationships that can more effectively unlock the shared value in online consumer information, few companies have focused attention on this area. The tendency is to deal with fundamental security issues and expect that consumers will move on to higher levels of trust by themselves. The fact that security is a precondition for broader trusted relationships, however, does not make it a driver to the next stage. The dynamic progression of digital trust in the consumer world takes the form of a hierarchy of interdependent requirements, as illustrated in figure 5-1.[3] Until the first-level requirement—a secure environment for interaction—is met, consumers will not be able to move on to the next level. Once a sense of security is established, however, it is no longer an important motivator in the interaction, and the consumer tends to pay more attention to Web site performance issues. If the interactions with a particular online company get bogged down in performance problems—the Web site is too slow to respond, too confusing to navigate, etc.—the user will be diverted from moving up to the next level of the trust hierarchy, convenant, until these problems are resolved. Once consumers are comfortable with performance, they are able to consider the terms of the information covenant represented by interaction with a particular online company.

Only when the consumer and the merchant agree on some basic parameters that govern how the information shared online will be used, will the consumer be motivated to participate actively in information exchange, and move on to the final stage of shared value. On the other hand, if the information covenant is never explicitly established the consumer lacks a fundamental element for effective information disclosure and ultimately for the highest stage of online trust, the realization of shared value by both parties in the relationship. This is in sharp contrast to the model for B2B information sharing discussed in chapter 4, where companies tend to begin exchanging information much more quickly. It's a difference that leads many managers to underestimate the challenge of gaining consumer trust.

A full discussion of each step in this digital trust hierarchy will clarify why meeting the challenges intrinsic to each level is essential but not sufficient to move consumers to the highest stage of shared value.

Security

Since security is the basic prerequisite for moving up the digital trust hierarchy and since online companies are almost universally ready to invest in basic security measures, it would seem that this step would be an easy one. But even at this level there are imbalances between the interests and priorities of the merchant and the needs of the customer. Companies typically focus their security efforts on protecting

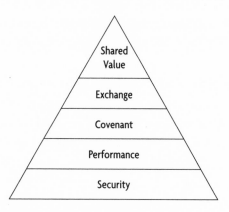

Figure 5-1 The Digital Trust Hierarchy for Consumers

against outside attacks and against fraud from customers. The worst case for a manager may be a Web shutdown or an embarrassing public break-in, and preventing such problems absorbs a lot of security attention. From the consumer point of view, these are annoying but not catastrophic problems. Consumers worry more about their personal identity and financial information being exposed to prying eyes—those inside the firm as well as outside. To move beyond this first level of the trust hierarchy, Web sites need to make it clear that the security preparations of the merchant are dedicated to protecting personal information from internal as well as external compromise, along with ensuring the overall integrity and protected access to the Web site itself.

Performance

The next level of the trust hierarchy involves the performance of the company online and how easy or difficult it is for the consumer to do business with it. This includes basics such as the consumer's ability to identify the purpose of the site, find what he or she is looking for, and consummate a transaction with the merchant. Such capabilities seem so obvious that every online merchant ought to pass with flying colors, but it turns out that many of them still do quite badly at the performance level. If it is hard to navigate the Web site, if the information on display is confusing or outdated, if there are broken links, or if material takes too long to download, customers are shown sloppy workmanship, which they will assume extends to unseen tasks such as the protection of personal information. These failings leave potential customers frustrated and lead them to abandon their shopping carts in mid-click and move on to another merchant or to reconsider the advantages of e-commerce altogether. A study of online consumer behavior cosponsored by Sapient and the Cheskin Research Group highlights the importance of meeting basic performance criteria as a step to building consumer trust. This "E-Commerce Trust Study" identified the following six factors as being the most directly related to establishing a positive sense of trust on the part of online consumers[4]:

Brand: Does the merchant have a recognizable brand?

Not surprisingly, brand recognition was the number one trust-generating factor for consumers. Consumers tended to rate the Web sites of well-known brands higher than the sites of lesser-known brands on a number of dimensions, including their willingness to place an order. But there was also good news in the study for emerging and less well-known companies. If their Web sites scored high on all the remaining factors, consumers were almost equally inclined to trust them at least to the extent of completing a transaction.

Navigation: Is the site easy and intuitive to use?

This emerged as the second most important factor in establishing trust, whether or not the company had a recognized brand. In other words, badly designed sites of bricks-and-mortar companies could cause them to lose ground in the eyes of the consumer. Consumers associated difficulty in finding what they were looking for and confusing graphics on a Web site with potential problems in dealing with the company running or sponsoring the site.

Fulfillment: Are the steps in the ordering, shipment, and dispute resolution processes clear?

Visitors wanted to see explicit information about what was going to happen if they placed an order or transacted other business with this company. Was there a follow-up alternative besides e-mail, such as a customer support phone number? Did the site clarify shipping and return options? There were a number of questions that visitors wanted to have answered before they placed an order—and not finding answers would be enough to prevent order completion.

Presentation: Does the site exhibit care and professionalism in its construction?

Even mundane lapses such as typos and broken links tend to downgrade the level of trust that the visitor is willing to place in a site. One assumption seems to be that if the merchant is careless with the details of presenting itself on the Internet, it might well be careless in fulfilling orders or protecting the consumer's personal information.

Up-to-Date Technology: Is the Web site responsive in terms of speed and interactive features?

The technology factors that make a difference to the visitor are those that relate most closely to the perceived performance of the site.

Seals of Approval: Is the merchant partnering with recognized organizations that review and endorse the performance of Web sites according to specific criteria?

In response to the demand for online trust, a number of nonprofit organizations, including TRUSTe and BBBonline (Better Business Bureau Online), have emerged to promote self-regulation by online companies and to promulgate agreed-on standards of conduct for managing customer information. Members that comply with these codes of conduct are entitled to display a seal of membership on their Web sites. Some specific recommendations of these organizations will be discussed in more detail later in this chapter. To the extent that the visitor is familiar with such programs, these seals are important in building consumer trust, especially for sites with less familiar brand names. Displaying the logos of credit card associations, on the other hand, does little to increase trust in a Web site.

If online companies fall down on one or more of these factors, then it is less likely that users will be motivated to return or to move up the trust scale to actively exchange information with this company. If all goes well, consumers now have enough experience and positive performance feedback to contemplate coming back again. This raises additional questions about what it will mean to extend their trust in relationship to this company. What is going to happen to the information they will share deliberately and inadvertently by dint of regular visits? What does this merchant do with the information that is collected? How does it protect it? These are the questions that must be answered at the covenant level of the digital trust hierarchy.

Covenant

At this stage of the trust hierarchy, consumers move from being observers and evaluators of online merchant performance to considering a more interactive relationship. In the business-to-business world we saw that this stage is fairly straightforward because the participating companies are already part of a marketplace that requires at least information exchange. The consumer, however, needs to be convinced that information exchange is a positive step and that the online merchant will treat the information with respect. Does the merchant have agreements with third parties or a collaborative to pool information that is being collected, either in aggregate form or through profiling of individual behavior? Companies have taken to including this type of information in a privacy policy that is linked to their home page. Unfortunately, most of these policies are written in dense legal language and are difficult to interpret. That makes it hard for the consumer to make a positive decision about information exchange.

Some companies display a privacy policy that emphasizes consumer protection, but they may report only the information protection

practices of the company itself and gloss over the fact that third parties will also be tracking online behavior and collecting information
about visitors to the site. These third-party agreements are often what
stir up consumer indignation. Other companies do not clarify all the
methods they use to collect information about their visitors. Obviously if the covenant is violated in any of these ways, the company will
lose the progress it has made in moving customers up the digital trust
hierarchy and will find it even more difficult than the first time
around to gain the customer's trust.

Information Exchange

At this stage consumers are satisfied with the basic security and performance of the online company and are confident that the treatment
of their personal data matches their expectations. They are ready to
begin exchanging more explicitly personal information with the company. This exchange may include volunteering more personal data for
registration, requesting news and personal information services such
as gift reminders, using applications such as financial planning tools,
or simply taking advantage of online organization and storage
options. Creation of a "My Yahoo!" or a "MySchwab" or other personalized Web page is a basic form of information exchange. Many
companies are basing their business models on reaching this level
of trust, because consumers that have entrusted information and
established a base of customized services are the most likely to return
regularly and to begin using other services from that company. One
of the big wins for companies that reach the exchange stage is that
individuals who have created personal information files on a particular Web site will be likely to return frequently to that site and be
exposed to the offers and ads for other services. Even more important, there will be barriers to moving all the information to another
site and starting all over again in building trust there. And, finally,
there are positive incentives to store other types of information and
to begin thinking of that online company as the provider of other
services.

Shared Value

At this top level of the trust hierarchy, the consumer and the merchant have established a basis for mutual trust and are ready to engage in a process for increasing returns based on the relationship. This is the stage of harvesting mutual value. As a reward for entrusting their financial record keeping to a personalized Quicken Web site, for example, Intuit might offer its customers a free or discounted copy of tax preparation software that can automatically upload the year's financial data from the customer desktop to a customized "My Taxes" page on Quicken. The customer has an easier time dealing with tax returns and decides to take advantage of the follow-up Intuit offer to store those returns on the Web for future access and tax planning. Once the customer accepts this offer, switching to another tax preparation package becomes unlikely, and buying into additional complementary products is almost guaranteed.

If customers are sharing in the control and the rewards of the use of their information, then more information will be provided and more business conducted. This moves the merchant beyond simply filling the customer's immediate online purchasing needs to becoming the keeper of the customer's Web-wide trust. The trusted merchant can realize revenue by becoming a trusted representative, confidant, and advisor to the customer. Who pays the merchant for this trust brokerage service? Both the customer—through sharing more and more information—and the other merchants who are eager to partner with the company to obtain direct access to loyal customers who are predisposed to extend their trust through established channels.

Spelled out step by step, the digital trust hierarchy may sound like a protracted process that takes too long to match the fast pace of the Internet. But these levels of trust do not have to be separated by weeks or even days. If a company has planned for building trust and has designed its Web site accordingly, consumers can move from performance to information exchange and shared value in just one or two visits. The problem is that most companies put unnecessary roadblocks in the customer's way in the form of poor online communication or site design. Instead of adapting their processes to the digital trust hierarchy, these companies tend to use various online technologies to simulate the top of the trust hierarchy and offer one-sided versions of personalized services. The next section discusses the attractions and the pitfalls of such an approach.

Unsatisfactory Shortcuts to Personal Information Pooling

Instead of meeting consumers halfway and moving with them through the digital trust hierarchy, companies may look for shortcuts to obtain massive amounts of information about present and potential customers all at once. If a company already operates a popular Web site, it can simply sit back and keep track of all visitor activities and link that information to online registration data or to records of previous Web visits. The company may turn this data into cash flow by using it to boost advertising revenues on its site. Even if the company Web site is not a magnet for millions of customers, managers can easily obtain detailed customer behavior information from other sites by signing up for an information-pooling service such as DoubleClick. Neither of these activities requires any permission or direct interaction with the individuals who are generating the information.

This approach may fulfill a company's short-term desire to amass lots of customer information and capitalize on it as quickly as possible, but it does nothing to deepen the trust relationship with the target consumers or to address their concerns about online information pooling. In fact, if this behind-the-scenes data collection is called to their attention, it may well alienate the very customers the company is working to profile.

But what if the company is not out to make a quick buck from customer traffic and instead wants to create personalized, targeted offers for its existing customers without bothering them with a direct request or overburdening them with the details of how online information is collected and analyzed? Isn't a more personalized Web site going to encourage return visits and create customer loyalty whether or not the customers took an active role in the personalization process? Convinced that instant personalization is essential for online success, many companies have bought into personalization tools that don't depend on customer participation. If these tools are used to enhance the Web site and the understanding of customer preferences, they may well provide a positive addition to management strategy. But they are not likely to create the level of customer loyalty or perceived value that their visitors are expecting.

Figure 5-2 maps the relationship between customer control of personalization and the perceived value of that information. Customers place the highest value on personalized, trusted services that are based in part on information they have voluntarily shared with the online service provider. This type of service also creates the highest switching cost, since the consumer would have to reestablish the trust as well as recreate the underlying information to move to a new provider. Even data from profiling, order-and-delivery requests, and convenience services can create a barrier to switching as long as the consumer has put in personal time creating the profiles. Data collected without customer knowledge, however, has almost no personal value.

A closer look makes it clear why personalization based on low levels of customer involvement and low customer control is less likely to create sustainable customer loyalty. The key difference is in the degree of control available to the customer. Individuals have a natural inclination to value what is under their own control over activities or messages that are controlled by others. In a world where customers are constantly bombarded by "personal" direct mail solicitations, phone calls, and now Web banners and e-mail messages, what stands out are those online services that the customer can call his own.

It may be hard for managers to resist a cornucopia of financial benefits that accrue to online companies from the passive data collection practices so widespread today. However, a relevant question is whether consumer trust and long-term relationships are likely to

	Degree of Customer Control / Switching Costs / Personal Value →	
Degree of Personalization ↑	**Personalized Marketing** (targeted offers, personalized selections, special discounts based on past shopping patterns)	**Personalized Trusted Services** (medical and financial advice, business and lifestyle services)
	Data Collected behind the Scenes (cookies, using embedded programs to track online behavior, DoubleClick information sharing)	**Data Disclosed to Add Convenience** (preregistration for ordering and delivery, profiling of special interests and news preferences)

Figure 5-2 The Value of Consumer Control of Online Information

increase based on these shortcuts to personalization. The answer is most likely to be no. As the digital trust hierarchy illustrates, any meaningful online personalization has to involve the active participation of the user and be based on trust. If companies start from a basis of trust, and both users and companies share information with a clear understanding about issues of control and access, then all parties to the transaction are going to be gratified by the return of extra value.

Businesses that gather and control consumer information and hoard all the rewards from its use reinforce consumer reluctance to entrust personal information to the Web and make the trust-building process more difficult for all Web merchants. There are two paths to overcoming this reluctance. Companies must give more explicit control over information pooling back to the individual, and they must increase the value generated for the customer. It may seem in the short run that both of these alternatives add to the complexity of doing business on the Web and limit the ability of the company to maximize its own value, but in the context of a digital value system the overall payback for this approach is enormous. If we think of the span of a trust as being the range of situations in which it can be used or deployed, then digital trust intrinsically demands a much greater span than bricks-and-mortar trust. This makes it more difficult to establish in the short run, but it provides significant advantages above and beyond bricks–and-mortar trust for those companies that do climb to the top of the trust hierarchy with their customers. For one thing, all this effort means that those firms that go through with it are likely to be among a small number of trusted digital brokers selected by customers.

Once a customer has invested in building a trusted relationship and is actively sharing information and receiving value from an online enterprise, that customer has multiple incentives to consolidate the activities that require trust under this existing umbrella. It matters less in the digital world where the trust got started—it could be a grocery store or a software company or an investment service. It is easier to expand digital trust from one domain to another than it is to start all over at the bottom of another pyramid as one is forced to do in the bricks-and-mortar world. This means that winning online trust early and continually expanding it will be extremely valuable over the lifetime of the customer. Losing it halfway up the pyramid, on the other hand, will be a major if not fatal setback. This is the risk that companies are taking when they try to short-circuit the trust hierarchy by using the Internet to collect and trade in personal information without the knowledge of the customer.

The Personal Privacy Backlash

Unfortunately, many of the companies that expect to thrive on the intake and resale of this valuable digital information asset don't take the time or the initiative to establish prior trust. Instead of creating new value relationships with the source of the information—the online customer—online merchants are all too often more eager to help themselves to as much profit as possible behind the scenes. Left to find out on their own that the rules of the game are different in the digital world, consumers have been understandably reluctant to share personal information without some assurances about trust, control, and privacy. The failure to establish a solid basis for trust and to properly motivate and reward the sharing of consumer information on the part of the consumer creates a potential roadblock to the well-being of the entire value system. This takes the form of a personal privacy backlash as more consumers become slowly, surely, and painfully aware of the ways of the Web.

In the end, Web merchants that persist in collecting information behind the scenes are inviting consumers to assert more control either by using Web tools to take ownership of and responsibility for controlling their own information or by demanding protection from an outside regulator with the clout to enforce consistent information practices. The latter approach seems to be the one taking hold as exposés about the treatment of personal online information by U.S. companies continue to mount.

In fact, more often than not, when companies have pooled information about their customers with other online merchants or tried to justify unreported online tracking and data collection about individual Web visitors, they have been treated to controversy and bad publicity when such practices were made public. There have been a number of very public missteps, stumbles, and vigorous backpedalings as firms seeking to extract the value in pooled consumer information found they had to extract themselves instead from the tar pits of advocacy group opprobrium and customer backlash.

Despite this clear evidence of consumer concern and potential backlash, however, companies persist in their online data collection and information-pooling practices. In fact, tracking and sharing data about consumer behavior on the Internet have spawned a growth industry with hundreds of companies developing the underlying tracking technologies and offering various types of information collection and targeted marketing services. Leaders in the field, such as DoubleClick, are now huge conglomerates in their own right. DoubleClick has paid more than a billion dollars to amass even more consumer information by acquiring firms such as Abacus Direct and Netgravity. These acquisitions give DoubleClick a window into millions of detailed individual offline catalog purchases, an overlap that has raised renewed concerns by consumer privacy watchdogs that Internet information pooling is taking on a Big Brother atmosphere.

The point is not whether any negative effects of online information pooling are likely to happen, but that individuals don't typically understand or feel they exercise any control over the personal information that is collected on the Web. This lack of control—this breaking down of the familiar and taken-for-granted firewalls between information stores—and the exponential increase in the size of the pool and who has access to it online are behind the negative reaction to disclosure of information-pooling or antiprivacy practices on the Web and will continue to fuel consumer dissatisfaction until resolved.

In Pursuit of Privacy on the Web

Clearly, the Web has been through many changes since Scott McNealy, Sun Microsystems CEO, made his position on the digital privacy debate absolutely clear by proclaiming to reporters, "You have zero privacy anyway. Get over it."[5] This statement, however, is not as negative as it might seem at first glance. The Internet, after all, started out and in large part remains an ingenious mechanism for worldwide information sharing, rather than privacy protection. One of its first applications was the file transfer protocol (ftp) that still underpins the movement of much online data around the globe. The whole point of the Web was to let scientists browse freely through other people's computer files to retrieve all the different bits of information that linked to a particular topic. In the early days of academic and research Internet use, a popular Unix utility called "finger" let anyone find out whether a user was currently online simply by fingering their Internet connected computer. Today's Internet is a vast elaboration and scaling up of these Stone Age tools and a prime hunting ground for all kinds of user information.

Debate continues about whether the tools and processes available for online companies to collect and share information about visitors—both in the aggregate and as individuals—constitutes an invasion of privacy. Even agreeing on the definition of privacy in the context of the Internet turns out to be a challenge. The willingness to share information about oneself is, not surprisingly, a very personal matter. For some people, the discovery that the Web form they filled out a few months ago has been circulated to affiliated companies is a clear breach of their privacy, while to others it is only to be expected and is no cause for concern, perhaps even desirable. For this group the news about information pooling on the Web may be a positive sign that online merchants care enough to try and personalize their messages based on previous browsing behavior.

Just as trust starts with a sense of control, it makes sense to think of online privacy in terms of giving control of personal information back to the individual. The element of control does in fact play a role in defining good online privacy practice. The OnLine Privacy Alliance, for example, a coalition of industry groups, defines the following guidelines for Web merchants to post privacy policies on their sites:

- Be easy to find, read, and understand.

- Provide consumers with information about what information is being collected and how it will be used.

- Provide information on how to exercise choice.

- Disclose the measures taken to assure the data's reliability.

- Provide a contact person to whom to communicate problems or concerns.

- Explain the mechanism to provide customers access to information to assure its accuracy.[6]

These guidelines adhere to the five core "fair information practice principles" for privacy protection that the U.S. government has established for itself and for the private sector in dealing with the collection and online maintenance of personal consumer data. The emphasis on consumer awareness, choice, and access reflect the need for individuals to exercise more conscious control over information sharing on the Web.

1. **Notice/Awareness:** Consumers must be given notice of a company's information practices before personal information is collected from them.

2. **Choice/Consent:** Consumers must be given options with respect to whether and how personal information collected from them may be used.

3. **Access/Participation:** Consumers must be given reasonable access to information collected about them and the ability to contest that data's accuracy and completeness.

4. **Integrity/Security:** Companies must take reasonable steps to assure that information collected from consumers is accurate and secure from unauthorized use.

5. **Enforcement/Redress:** Government and/or self-regulatory mechanisms must be in place to impose sanctions for noncompliance with fair information practices.[7]

The most important definition of privacy, however, is the one in the mind of the individual customer who visits a merchant's Web site. If the dialogue between customer and merchant includes a full disclosure of the information collection practices and the benefits of that Web site, and if the individual agrees to participate on those terms, the stage is set for trust and exchange of value. The terms of the information sharing are not nearly as important as the principle of mutual agreement and control. But when companies violate the terms of that original dialogue, consumer trust quickly evaporates.

A comparison of two sites that facilitate access to online music illustrates this point. RealNetworks has an excellent reputation for its audio software and attracts millions of visitors by posting free software for playing digital music on its Web site for downloading onto the desktop. In the fall of 1999, hundreds of thousands of satisfied users had already installed a new piece of RealNetworks software called the RealJukebox when a user who also happened to be a computer expert noticed that his RealJukebox seemed to be in regular, independent communication with the RealNetworks home server. Some computer sleuthing revealed that this free software that was residing on desktops around the world had some unannounced information collection and reporting features.[8]

RealJukebox was tracking all the music that was downloaded from the Net and played and sending back a regular report to the RealNetworks server. To make matters worse, the software had a unique serial number that could easily be linked with the personal information that users sent to RealNetworks when they registered for support and site access. The news that a well-respected and very popular Web site was busy collecting data about the music downloading and listening habits of named individuals struck many users as a step too far into their privacy zone. The CEO of RealNetworks quickly issued a public apology and promised that the company would do better in regard to privacy in the future. It also issued a patch to allow users to disable the tracking functions of RealJukebox. But a great deal of damage was done.

Napster.com, in contrast, allows users to share their personal digital music cuts via an open file sharing system.[9] By registering to participate and downloading the Napster software, each user is in effect agreeing to join Napster's distributed computer music network. Napster tracks the music files in specific directories on each user's computer, and these files are completely visible to other Napster users. It is possible to search an individual's personal music files and grab music for downloading at will. The curious user can also browse around the Napster network just to see what people are collecting or downloading at any given time. But the participants don't object to this degree of information exposure because they have consciously signed on to the system, and they perceive that the value of the music they receive in exchange more than balances the pooling of information and music resources on their part.

Napster's experience with its customers is a good illustration of the willingness to share that, by and large, still characterizes individual Internet users. The valuable information harvest is still available to Internet merchants if they pick the fruit gently. That is what makes building in consumer choice and control over information sharing such a good investment for Web merchants. With full disclosure and an appropriate motivational incentive, many consumers will tell everything the merchant wants to know and a lot more. And there will be no backlash problem to worry about down the road.

Conclusion

Taking responsibility for the consumer's information-pooling interests is not just an added cost of doing business on the Internet. It is an enhanced business opportunity. It creates a new form of trust relationship we call digital trust, which presents new value opportunities for both the business that earns the trust and the consumer who grants it.

Digital trust is not confined to procedures surrounding encrypted files or PIN-protected accounts. It is not limited to use in carefully controlled situations nor is it defined in endless paragraphs of small-print legalese. It is a tacit convergence of common interests, a seeing eye to eye, a rapport if you will, built up through daily or weekly interactions and experiences that lead the consumer to trust an online resource. Without this convergence, online companies will face an uphill battle in turning all the consumer information that can be harvested from the Web into sustainable and revenue-generating relationships.

Once they move onto the Internet, consumers become active, if initially unwilling, participants in the market's information pool. In the absence of strict regulations about the treatment of personal information on the Net, businesses have been free to take advantage of—some would say abuse—their access to a rich new vein of consumer data. Companies are becoming more and more efficient at harvesting and sharing the aggregate information that Web visitors contribute to the pool and at pinpointing individual behavior and preferences. For the most part, the consumers who generate all this new data are not allowed to control its use nor reap any direct rewards for their contribution. As the new members of this digital value system start to react to the appropriation of their default trust by either withdrawing from the pool or threatening government regulation of the pool, smart businesses will realize that they have more to lose than gain by not taking into account the information-pooling demands and requirements of consumers.

Reputation takes on a far greater importance in the Internet economy. The goodwill that is currently carried on a company's books as an accounting nicety will be given a much more realistic valuation by the online marketplace. As the vendors on eBay have discovered, reputation has a direct relationship to sales. Indeed, the role of reputation in driving the success of the dot-com businesses is a harbinger of things to come for businesses many, many times their size. A reputation gained will be fiercely protected because of its incredible value and because a reputation lost will be very, very hard to regain.

Digital trust changes behavior. There is a feedback loop in trusting and being trusted. Trust also solidifies relationships. Trust is hard to build and thus is an incentive to not switching. Take-it-all sites will ultimately lose out to sites that have both trust and information and so are able to move on to the next stage of building relationships. The issue is engaging the consumer in the control of the information and in sending some of the value back to the consumer. One way to accomplish this is to establish a balance between respect for individual privacy and desire for meaningful online personalization. Finally, the trust between the consumer and the business will expand to cover features of their relationship that were only implicit in their bricks-and-mortar relationship. This will be the focus of chapter 6.

CHAPTER SIX

The Power of
Exponential Relationships

As Internet-based companies and entrepreneurs spin more and more innovations off into the marketplace, it has become almost impossible to keep track of the emerging opportunities, never mind predict the potential winners. On the Net, the number of "new new things" expands exponentially as each new idea partners with each of the others and the life span of the losing technologies grows shorter and shorter.[1] Online offerings can penetrate the marketplace more quickly than ever, but that does not necessarily mean they will translate into profitable business models or popular favorites. The fact remains that technology alone cannot ensure loyalty—customers have to see some personal value in the innovation before they will embrace it. And predicting which innovations will take the market by storm has been fraught with more misses than hits.

By spawning eyeball-hungry competitors from unexpected quarters and pushing the pace of technology development, the Internet poses tough challenges to managers who are trying to figure out what their customers really want. At the same time, this global network offers a vast and constantly expanding market to companies that have developed an integrated digital value system. Advanced Web sites can simultaneously manage millions of casual visitors, recognize returning customers, provide different types of content and interactive pathways depending on individual preferences and past browsing histories, and do it all in a trusted, relationship-building mode by getting the individual to actively contribute to the process. Managing real-time relationships via the Internet provides opportunities to create customer buy-in and loyalty that most managers haven't fully grasped and few companies have built into their customer-facing strategies.

The core elements that enable this transformation in online relationships are collectively defined in this chapter as the "PER effect," or the power of exponential relationships. The PER effect is part of a dynamic cycle that generates more and more trusted relationships within the digital value system framework, providing the impetus for new product developments and for designing service offerings that allow companies to keep ahead of the wave in the ever-changing Internet economy. The power of exponential relationships means that the more participation and exchanges that take place within a value system, the more value there is available to each individual participant, including the following:

- a shift from passive to interactive to real-time product experiences as customers take the initiative to personalize and share information with other users and with the company in a variety of integrated online and offline contexts; and

- the ability to test ideas and products, get broad market feedback, and move more quickly in response to new technology and opportunities with a focus on serving customer communities by bringing them inside the digital value system.

This chapter analyzes how the PER effect transforms strategy for building customer relationships from a resource-constrained, company-driven process to a shared and unlimited exchange of increasing value in an open marketplace. Exponential relationship building represents a fundamental shift in how managers need to think about generating and providing value for customers. Companies that don't have a comprehensive strategy for building and enhancing online real-time customer relationships will find themselves increasingly shut off from the prime source for vital information about customer needs and expanding markets.

The More, the Better

Like some digital Rumplestiltskin spinning straw into gold, strategically managed, trusted Web sites can turn enormous numbers of visitors and large rates of participation into high-quality individual relationships. Given the right tools, the more people who join a digital value system, the better the level of individualization that any one customer is likely to receive. The shared data grows richer and the total pool of resources keeps expanding as more people take advantage of a particular online service or Web site. This may sound irresistible in theory, but does it really work in practice? Consider an exponential relationship effect that took the online music world by storm—a modest program for sharing MP3 digital music files called Napster. In chapter 5, we analyzed Napster's relationship to the digital trust hierarchy and concluded that individual consumers could see the value of open information sharing as long as they were able to exercise control over the degree of their participation and reap tangible benefits. In terms of exponential relationship value, it is also worth examining how this program grew from dozens to millions of online users by leveraging the resources of its participants.

Napster combines a simple plan with the power of the Internet to connect people and resources in real time. Picture a user-friendly, point-and-click, free software package for acquiring your favorite music tracks, playing them through your computer's sound system, and storing them on your hard drive for future listening. Add an equally simple system for searching a vast online inventory of digital music by song title or artist and downloading it to your personal files whenever you want. Now connect the personal computers of all the people who are using this software to a cluster of Internet servers so that everyone can browse and help themselves to everyone else's music files. What you get is a system that can grow at an exponential rate with very little central support and increasing returns for all participants as the size of the user base skyrockets.

Napster represents a breakthrough in exponential relationship value rather than a technical tour de force. In fact, the technology behind Napster is simply an application of the well-known and well-worn file-sharing capabilities of the Internet that go back to ftp, the basic file transfer protocol of the Net. The undergraduate who originally designed and released Napster was new to software development and used only a few basic programming tools found in any off-the-shelf program development package. The real power of Napster is its ability to handle millions of users interacting with each other in real time through the Internet's multiple interconnected servers, and transparent, peer-to-peer relationships between all participants.

Instead of high-powered technical innovation, the essence of the Napster value proposition is share and share alike. Users get access to the music on other people's computers in exchange for opening up parallel access to their own files. Whenever they log onto the Napster service, they become providers as well as consumers of resources. And the more they participate, the more they have available to share with the rest of the community the next time around. Once users come to terms with the security and performance issues of the Napster system and buy into this covenant for mutual exchange of resources, they are poised to add value to everyone else in the system. The workings of the system and its shared value proposition are so obvious that the consumer buy-in process is usually straightforward and swift—the steps from discovery of the resource and its covenant (the individual user "gets it") to security and performance evaluation (the user "wants it") to full resource sharing (the user "does it") can take place in rapid sequence.

Each member brings new resources to the system and helps to spread the load so that the system can accommodate more and more demand. As more users join the party, Napster becomes a growth and resource-aggregation juggernaut. Leaving legal and business questions aside for the moment, the growth of such a program is limited only by the size of the Internet itself. In the first nine months of its existence, word of mouth and online publicity fueled Napster's growth from a handful of college student users and a few hundred digital music tracks into a distributed resource encompassing millions of music files and more than 500,000 active users. By the time network administrators on college campuses took note of a massive spike in downloading activity and tried to shut off access to Napster for their students, regular users were devoted enough to circulate petitions and lead demonstrations to save their Napster access. Such spontaneous growth and loyal user communities underscore the disruptive power of new value relationships in an interconnected world.

Along the way, Napster, of course, incurred the wrath of many established players in the music industry. The recording industry filed suit claiming copyright infringement for the prerecorded music that users were exchanging on Napster. Legal battles may well prevent Napster from turning itself into a profitable business, but they don't detract from its demonstration that "more is better" when it comes to relationships and resources on the Internet. The Napster concept applies to any type of digital resource, and other companies are already launching similar programs for software and video file sharing, using a server-to-server distribution model. It won't be long before new business models and the tide of online users who buy into them become major forces in the Internet economy.

Harnessing the PER Effect for Business

Other examples of exponential relationship power have already been harnessed by leading Internet enterprises for competitive advantage. The appeal of information pooling of stock picks and investment strategies has spawned dozens of companies that bring together analyst reports and community discussion groups focused on the stock market. The model adopted by Clearstation, now an E*TRADE subsidiary, combines the intrinsic appeal of discussing investment picks with a more structured system for leveraging the power of active and widespread participation. The Clearstation investment site makes it simple for every new member to establish a personal portfolio to track the performance of stocks and collect information about companies of interest, including the comments of all other members. These portfolios are a free and private service designed to help individuals track stocks easily and keep track of the value of their holdings while considering new investment moves. Taking the information-pooling model one step further, Clearstation also lets members share a public "recommended" list of investments with the rest of the community. These recommended lists carry with them a history of how the picks have performed over time, which in effect provides a ranking of the financial astuteness of the member who selected them. A link to the top-performing recommended lists is available on the Clearstation home page so the members can see who is making the best choices and perhaps elect to follow that lead.

This model allows Clearstation to compress the value of the best insights from among all of its members and to present it to the collective. The more people who participate, the more data about which stocks and which recommenders are most successful over time become available to members and the more grist they have available to inform their own financial choices.

Taking a different approach to exponential relationship power, AOL's popular Instant Messaging system has helped to differentiate the network's own communication services and has been built into customer support systems and business-to-business applications. The origins of Instant Messaging, like those of Napster, demonstrate that facilitating simple connections among Internet users can have far-reaching benefits. The Instant Messaging story started in Israel, when two software engineers had an inspiration about putting real-time communication protocols that had been around since the dawn of the Internet to a new use. Their prototype product, called ICQ, featured an engaging Web browser interface that allowed anyone who downloaded the

ICQ software to send a quick message to any friend who signed up for the ICQ network. The interesting feature of this message was that it could pop up instantly on the computer screen of the recipient if the addressee was already logged onto the Net. Rather than try to sell the software commercially, the designers decided to distribute it for free on the Net.

Two years later ICQ had more than 50 million users around the world and a corporate valuation in the millions even though the company was giving away the product for free. ICQ users weren't classic customers—no one had asked them to pay for anything, and often no one except a friend had "marketed" the ICQ service to them. For the most part ICQ users identified with their own personal cluster of friends rather than with the network as a whole. But collectively, the expanding user base created a communication network that could speed traffic around the world and could add more and more new members who could then find more people they wanted to reach immediately. That, in turn, was enough to convince AOL to pay $280 million to acquire ICQ and build it into the Instant Messaging Service.

ICQ took the open standards of the Internet and used them to create a service that was tailor-made for Net users, made it easy enough to use so that people could help themselves to it, and took advantage of viral marketing by building in an incentive for every user to encourage their friends to join. The Internet was simultaneously the total market and the sole marketing tool. ICQ combined the value of personalized messages with the instant gratification of real-time interaction with people and the option of paging them through the Web. Most important of all, it turned the familiar, sequential exchange of e-mail into a real-time, interactive experience that could grow at Internet speed.

The PER effect allows companies to build high-value relationships with individual business and consumer customers and at the same time to listen to the broader marketplace. By moving from superficial formulas for online personalization to direct communication with online customers, managers can use the Web to bridge the reach and responsiveness gap that limits relationship building in other media.

Putting the power of exponential relationships to work allows companies to do the following:

- let customers take the initiative in building the business-to-consumer relationship up to a level of trust and fulfillment that provides both the business and the customer with optimal value;

- expand the digital value system to provide a scan of the broader marketplace for themselves and for their partners;

- use real-time interaction to constantly test new offers across a range of relationships and market segments;

- improve and adjust offers in real time to keep up with changes in demand; and

- anticipate what is coming next in terms of potential customers for different types of services and products.

Real-time interactions with all online customers expand a company's market reach to include the broader universe of potential customers who are connected to the Internet. Equally important, the PER effect represents a critical inversion of the bricks-and-mortar business assumptions about and experience of high value customer relationship management. Unlike the bricks-and-mortar world, where service and satisfaction tend to decrease as traffic and transaction volume increase, the Net-based commercial offerings can actually improve in quality as more people accept them and contribute resources to them. This heralds an end to the traditional trade-off between the number of customers that can be served and the depth and quality of the service provided—another facet of "the more, the better."

There have always been premier customer groups—the cream of the cream, high-profit generators that companies would go out of their way to cultivate through personalized services. But it was a challenge simply to identify that group of regular spenders and to track their behavior patterns and anticipate their needs. Even those companies that pride themselves on personalized services could not manage to keep close track of more than a few hundred thousand such customers, and most elite lists were much smaller.

But over the past five years, the Internet has demonstrated that given enough information and trust, many customers who fit the classic high-value profile of an educated, well-off consumer, actually prefer to make purchases online. What's more, as long as the numbers don't slow down response time, Web sites can make a virtue of attracting a crowd of visitors. Online markets such as eBay thrive because they bring together a critical mass of buyers and sellers, which guarantees a brisk trade and a steady flow of new goods on offer. The value of any auction or brokerage site is enhanced by a large flow of visitors to ensure liquidity. Similarly, the aggregation of experts and practitioners on a targeted discussion or community site, such as the technology-oriented Usenet newsgroup of old, brings more value by expanding the resources available to respond to questions and by creating a sense of community. The huge customer base selecting books at Amazon or downloading music from MP3.com feeds a stream of valuable data to the database and software engines that constantly sort and match selections to customer profiles behind the scenes. This, in turn, contributes to the accuracy with which those sites can target recommended titles to match the taste of any individual visitor.

Eliminating the traditional trade-off between broad reach and in-depth customer relationships changes all the rules for marketing and customer services. Internet-based relationship management offers any size company the optimal combination of high reach and high responsiveness at a realistic cost/staffing ratio. Instead of dividing attention between current high-value customers and potential new markets, companies with a fully elaborated digital value system in place can share information and track developments at many levels simultaneously. The entire Internet becomes a powerful market-tracking tool as well as a channel for communication and relationship building, far eclipsing any tools that managers have had at their disposal previously.

The Relationship Gap

It would be misleading to imply that the majority of high-traffic corporate Web sites are doing a good job of real-time relationship management today. In fact, most sites don't even measure up to the basic
expectations for providing timely feedback to online visitors. A report
by Rubric, an e-commerce software provider, cited repeated failures
to capitalize on opportunities to build interactive relationships at
some of the Web's most popular sites. Rubric gave fifty people $50
each to make a purchase at an e-commerce Web site chosen from
among the top fifty most visited sites and recorded the performance
of each site on a number of relationship-building measures.

The study focused on some basic relationship best practices,
including cross-selling and follow-up e-mail to interested shoppers,
second-stage personalization such as greeting return customers by
name, and tailoring content to match previously expressed interests.
Among the findings were the following:

Communication: Only about half of the sites surveyed tried to cross-
sell products by asking customers if they would like to receive
information on related items. And of the few sites that did get out
follow-up e-mails, 84 percent did not make the 30-day deadline,
widely considered optimal.

Personalization: Many opportunities to personalize e-commerce were
also missed. Follow-up e-mails and content on return visits were
infrequently tailored to the interests of a particular shopper. More-
over, only one in twenty-five sites personalized messages, and only
one in four recognized repeat buyers.

Customer service: While 57 percent of the sites offered a self-service
means of checking on an order's status, 40 percent didn't even
respond to e-mail order inquiries.[2]

Clearly, there is an enormous gap between the Internet's technical
potential to deliver highly personalized, dynamic, and value-rich services and the actual experience of today's Internet users at most Web

sites. Some of the barriers to realizing this potential spring from inflexible IT infrastructures at large corporations, and some come from the intrinsic difficulty and expense of keeping up with Internet growth rates and designing Web sites that are robust and flexible enough to keep up with demand. But most of the gap is strategic in nature. Managers haven't implemented a comprehensive and integrated framework for optimizing their company's online value—in other words, they don't have a digital value system. Far from turning every online customer into a source of increasing value, the companies that don't respond to e-mail or deepen the personalization on their Web sites are holding the door wide open for online competitors to lure their customers away. The gap between Web potential and actual practice is still large enough to quickly drive any number of relationship-savvy contenders to the top of the customer value charts in emerging and existing industries.

One company that has seized this opportunity in health care information is Mediconsult.com. A close look at its strategic balance of information, trust, relationships, and services illustrates how these four elements, through their interconnections, fuel company growth and attract both partners and customers to a new digital value system.

What could be more personal than individual health concerns and medical questions? It might seem that many health problems would be too sensitive for discussion and treatment advice on the Web, but in fact the consumer demand for online health information seems to be insatiable. Health-related Web sites are one of the fastest growing and most frequently visited categories of online content. But only a handful of the thousands of Web-based health companies have managed to create a viable e-business model that generates increasing returns for all participants. Mediconsult.com aims to be one of those few by leveraging the power of exponential relationships in a trusted online environment.

Ian Sutcliffe, president of Mediconsult, emphasizes that his company has connected different stakeholders in health care since its founding in 1996: "We have focused on becoming a connection point for consumers, health care providers, and pharmaceutical companies.

From the consumer point of view, there is an overwhelming amount of information and a pressing need for a trusted source that will help to sort through the most important insights and put them in touch with support groups and experts to answer specific questions. From a pharmaceutical point of view, it is extremely valuable to find a platform for interacting with motivated, self-selected individuals who have a direct interest in finding out about treatments. Hospitals and health care providers are looking for ways to follow up with patients and encourage them to take the initiative for wellness. Mediconsult connects with all of these groups."[3]

In contrast to the lackluster performance reported in the Rubric study, Mediconsult makes an explicit promise that every e-mail will be answered within twenty-four hours. Visitors can sign up for a personalized, weekly e-mail newsletter. Enticements to real-time interaction and community building are prominent on each of the company's networks of health-related Web sites. The commitment to individual users is summed up by a prominent "Visitor Bill of Rights," spelling out Mediconsult's covenant with users (see "The Mediconsult Network Visitor Bill of Rights").

This proactive approach to information, trust, and relationships has made Mediconsult the most "sticky" of the health care information services, motivating users to stay an average of 13.7 minutes on the site per visit and to consult more than eleven pages of information. This compares to an average duration of 3 to 6 minutes per visit at other health care sites. Visitor loyalty is high, with a large percentage of return.

Its success in attracting highly motivated and segmented consumer and health specialist traffic to the Mediconsult community has allowed the company to craft lucrative sponsorship and e-business partnerships. Novartis, for example, sponsors a site dedicated to smoking cessation that is highly personalized to stimulate behavior modification as well as to promote its own branded medicine for kicking the nicotine habit. The Mediconsult-designed site encourages users to sign on for the complete program, including a personal roadmap for success, an online buddy, daily e-mails, and other motivators. Sutcliffe

THE MEDICONSULT NETWORK VISITOR BILL OF RIGHTS

The following principles are the standards that we have set for ourselves to better meet your expectations of service and quality from our network. This is our commitment to you:

1. All of the Mediconsult Network Web sites, communities, and technologies will support a superior visitor experience.

2. All of the Mediconsult sites provide serious, in-depth, trusted information and interactive tools across the most common chronic medical conditions.

3. All content adheres to sound editorial principles and utilizes the provision of evidence-based content from peer-reviewed sources.

4. All users can expect active and professionally monitored online communities—bulletin boards, chat, live events—where they will be treated with compassion and respect.

5. All editorial content is unbiased and is free from influence of sponsors or advertisers.

6. Mediconsult will provide full and complete disclosure of sponsor and advertising relationships.

7. All sponsorship programs are designed to add value to the visitor experience.

8. All visitors can expect the utmost privacy as outlined in our published privacy policy.

9. All Mediaconsult sites provide consistent navigation that takes the visitor as quickly and intuitively as possible to the information or services sought.

10. All visitors can expect that general help and support queries will be answered within 24 hours by a Mediconsult professional.[4]

emphasizes that the relationship between the program and its sponsor is clearly indicated up front and that participants are well informed about any information that is collected based on their participation. Those who sign on have made the assessment that the value they receive is a good exchange for the information provided to the sponsor: "We have listened carefully to the 4.5 million patients and doctors who visit our site monthly, and they have clearly indicated that they prefer on-site-sponsored programs to traditional advertising banners. Sponsorship programs that provide real value to these visitors have proven very popular."[5]

Recognizing that communication between physicians and patients is a fundamental component of health care, Mediconsult has designed innovative programs to foster this interaction online. Doctors can send regular e-mail reminders to their patients about taking prescribed medication or scheduling follow up appointments. Patients with chronic conditions are encouraged to fill out online questionnaires that provide their physician with important insights into their health maintenance between office visits.

Mediconsult illustrates its value proposition to sponsors and potential partners by showing how Internet-based interactions reduce the cost of patient education and behavior modification without sacrificing the patient's sense of personal service or trust. The average cost of a one-on-one visit with a health specialist, for example, is $50, while the average cost of a physical group behavior modification program is $30 per participant per session. Furthermore, the self-reported results from participants who stuck with the online, personalized version of the smoking cessation program were better than the results of a similar group registered for a traditional bricks-and-mortar program on an outpatient basis—and at a cost of only $3 per participant per session.

The company's ability to generate trust and build high-quality relationships by sharing health information illustrates that even complex digital value systems can be successful. But Mediconsult's own survey of competitive medical sites reinforces the conclusion of the

Rubric study: there is a huge gap between the potential for online relationship formation and the practice of most online enterprises. Of one hundred e-mail questions directed at medical information sites, the Mediconsult survey team received only twelve responses, a dismal rate of return in an area so dependent on building trust and relationships with users. The quality of the responses was even worse— eight of the twelve were automated, precanned answers, and only four were customized to reflect the particular interests of the questioner. The bottom line—out of a hundred questions, the survey turned up just two answers that were directly relevant to the original query. Sutcliffe sums up the Mediconsult competitive advantage: "Service and quality on the Internet are relatively rare."

That is an understatement for the first generation of the so-called personalized Web sites. But more and more companies are taking steps to reinvent themselves and their online offers to present more visible value to the customer. The next sections look in more detail at how to move from superficial customization to a high-value online customer relationship strategy.

Stages of Increasing Value

There are four stages of customer interaction that combine to broaden reach and expand individual responsiveness and reward. Figure 6-1 illustrates these stages, from information-based, mass personalization to interactive profiling to transactions based on trust to recurring shared value. At each stage, the customer becomes more directly involved with setting the parameters of the relationship and determining the level of personal disclosure. This, in turn, creates a positive feedback loop and increases the value of the next level of interactions.

The amount of shared information and trust correlates with the persistence and depth of the relationship and also with the particular stage that the customer has reached.

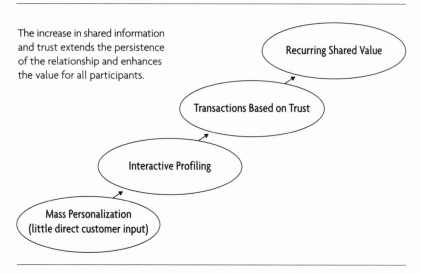

The increase in shared information and trust extends the persistence of the relationship and enhances the value for all participants.

Figure 6-1 Moving Online Relationships toward Increasing Value

Stage One: Mass Personalization

As the Rubric study and the Mediconsult survey have clearly shown, today's Web sites don't even begin to take advantage of the relationship potential they have. Tools to track site navigation and click streams are cheap and ubiquitous, enabling even the smallest start-up to compile an impressively complex visitor log file. Larger corporations can sign on with DoubleClick or other collaborative tracking services to obtain even more comprehensive data on aggregate and individual behavior patterns. But as companies are sucking up all types of data about customer online behavior, very few are returning any value to the individual customer. At best, the information is used to customize advertising and special offers to match the general profile that has been established for the customer. While these targeted marketing programs may stimulate higher click-through rates for advertisers, they don't do much to provide tangible rewards to the individual or to build a foundation for return visits or closer relationships. The limited amount of personalization generated by tracking online behavior does not compensate for the fact that companies are still treating the customers in batch mode and frequently not even using follow-up e-mail or return visits effectively to build up a sense of intensifying relationship. In other words, most companies would be better off investing in the resources needed in order to answer their e-mail promptly and effectively.

Not only are the benefits of mass personalization fairly limited, they can become a customer disincentive. To the extent that sites do not clarify their information-gathering practices and provide some opportunity for user control, they become part of the untrusted Web. As we saw in chapter 5, behind-the-scenes data collection programs run the risk of alienating visitors and short-circuiting the trust that is so essential for moving on to a higher-value relationship.

Stage Two: Interactive Profiling

Initiation of active customer involvement marks the critical turning point between stage one and stage two of online relationship building. Engaging the visitor in the personalization process increases the quality of the information that can be collected and opens the door to more highly valued services. Customers choose to share information and fill out profiles in exchange for some services or other incentive, and so the terms of the relationship are more advanced, and the level of the information released tends to be significantly higher. Once the individual customer takes an active role managing the information profile and adjusting it on a regular basis, his or her awareness of the relationship expands, as does the merchant's opportunity to offer related products and services. At the same time, the self-service aspect of interactive profiling allows Web-based companies to scale their personalization to meet the demands of the market.

Interactive profiling is still a long way from a full digital value relationship in most cases, however. Thousands of profile-based Web sites have been stuck at stage two and subsequently have fallen by the wayside. Until trust is introduced into the relationship at stage three, users can easily substitute one personalized Internet-based service for another.

StageThree: Transactions Based on Trust

The value of a relationship and the amount of trust that is placed in it typically increase in the bricks-and-mortar world as the personalization, level of investment on the part of the customer, and individual attention on the part of the merchant go up. The same is true in the online world: once interactions with a particular site are based on trust, the customer's willingness to extend the online relationship into future activities increases dramatically. Trust is an essential component of customer loyalty and the basis of delivering a variety of enhanced value-added services. As trust grows through experience, the customer shares even more information and participates in more e-services, creating a cycle of increasing value and responsiveness.

One example of the positive relationship feedback that can be built around trusted offers comes from the Dell Computer online order page. Like many strategically designed order sites, Dell's site provides a "Save the Cart" feature for its visitors. As we have seen, a large number of Internet users will browse through a Web site, select items, place them in a shopping cart, and then leave the site without completing the order process. Improved site design and higher trust will reduce the percentage of unconsummated orders, but there are still a fair number of shoppers who simply want to take more time before making the final commitment. This is especially true in the complex and rapidly changing field of computers and peripherals. Allowing customers to save their shopping carts on the site provides an incentive for them to come back later and take advantage of the selection efforts that they have already made.

Dell took "Save the Cart" one very interesting step further. It lets the hesitant customer set a password on the saved cart and choose to send it along to others with a personalized message. With the password in hand, friends or colleagues can access the original shopper's cart, look over the selections that have already been made, and either send some suggestions via e-mail or make adjustments directly to the items in the cart. This additional outside advice can be instrumental in validating a certain selection and moving the transaction toward completion. The people involved might be personal friends with some expertise in system configuration, colleagues who are going to share use of the system, or corporate IT personnel who have to support the system. The circle of trust is up to the individual customer, but obviously it includes Dell. Dell lets its customers leverage the trust built into their Web site to create tiny, transient information pools protected by passwords within which you can not only share information with others but also accumulate their advice.

Stage Four: Recurring Shared Value Cycles

With increasing participation and involvement by the customer, all the parties to an ongoing series of transactions can begin to rely on trusted, cumulative information that is always current and available to inform the next online activity. This stage of relationship has to incorporate both online and offline information and keep updates on all transactions in both realms. Along with its "One-Click" ordering to simplify the initial buy decision, for example, Amazon has also created a system of order fulfillment that incorporates rapid and continuous feedback on the status of the order to enhance the sense of relationship between customer and vendor. Not only does Amazon remember customer shipping preferences and alternate destination addresses, it keeps track of the progress of each part of the order.

Instead of traditional, one-on-one service in the bricks-and-mortar world, online customers demand instant gratification and personalization in the Web world. They tend to favor self-service as long as it truly saves them time and satisfies their needs, but they are quickly turned off by any lack of online responsiveness. Online customers expect multisided, real-time interaction to provide direct and visible value, such as customization of everything they need from A to Z.

This process generates increasing returns to the Web site and to the customer, as more fulfillment cycles take place and more services are offered at the point of online interaction. Each successful repetition builds trust and increases the store of customer-related information and preferences. The more the customer gains from each repeat visit, the more return they offer the value system providers in terms of lifetime loyalty, purchases, and information pooling.

Solving the Innovator's Dilemma

Bridging the gap between potential and realized relationship value is critical to online competition today. Companies cannot expect to keep customers loyal or understand the market demand for new products and services without constant information feedback and interaction with a growing community of customers. In fact, in the Internet economy, companies will eventually go out of business without this feedback and interaction. As we have seen in the previous chapters, information and trust are important components of a digital value system, but the real payoff comes when companies use the insights gleaned from information pooling and online interactions to build closer relationships with their customers. Relationships drive online growth, and as companies rapidly attract new users, trusted and information-rich relationships are vital to keeping current users loyal and to deepening as well as broadening the product and service offerings.

Over the years companies have spent huge amounts of time and money trying to crack the perennial puzzle of what customers really want in hopes of delivering it faster and better than the competition. The rhetoric attached to this goal has changed over time to be sure, as have the tools and techniques used to pursue it. Companies may alternately focus on quality of services or on exceeding customer expectations to ensure a "delighted customer." Managers work to integrate their IT strategies and systems data with the customer-facing points of contact to create a "360-degree" profile as a way to understand the total customer. Behind the scenes, they install customer relationship management (CRM) software to automate the process of collecting and mining data. Formulas calculate the customer's lifetime value and compare the cost of new customer acquisition with the investment required for higher retention rates. Mass customization gives way to one-to-one marketing as the method for catering to individual interests and personalizing product offers.

Because of the popularity of the Net, it has become simultane-ously more urgent and more challenging to figure out a winning for-mula for attracting and retaining customers. Web sites put increas-ing emphasis on personalization of marketing messages as the road to establishing a closer relationship with online customers. Interactive options proliferate as companies work to increase the stickiness of their sites and entice visitors to linger and buy. All of the these activi-ties, from quality management to Web marketing, converge on the assumption that the more a company knows about its customers, the more responsive it can be to their needs, leading to customer value, loyalty, and long-term profitability.

Recently, however, the reigning assumption that close customer relationships are fundamental to corporate success has come under more critical scrutiny. It turns out that executives' inability to pre-dict and prepare for the migration of customer value from mini-computers to PCs or from motion pictures to television broadcasts may stem at least in part from listening too closely to customers. As Clayton Christensen has documented in his research on the microelectronics and computer hardware industries, the stronger the ties to current customers, the more difficult it seems to be for companies to make changes in the product offerings and business models that might threaten those ties.

The inherent contradiction between meeting today's market demands and simultaneously keeping up with the innovations that are likely to launch emerging markets is at the heart of Christensen's book *The Innovator's Dilemma*. After reviewing the experience of market leaders over the past several decades, Christensen concludes that close customer relationships are not a panacea and may even become a problem in keeping up with changes in the market. When new products are being developed and adopted all around them, sooner or later well-established companies that are only tuned in to their existing customer base will get blindsided by disruptive tech-nologies that come up through a totally different market base.

In fact, according to Christensen, the more that managers focus their efforts and corporate resources on satisfying their leading customers, the less likely they will be able to anticipate fundamental market and technology shifts.

> Good resource allocation processes are designed to weed out proposals that customers don't want. When these decision-making processes work well, if customers don't want a product, it won't get funded; if they do want it, it will. This is how things must work in great companies. They must invest in things customers want—and the better they become at doing this, the more successful they will be.[6]

This tendency can loom as a double whammy for companies struggling to retain their existing customers and trying to figure out where the next wave of technology adoption will take hold. Should market leaders stick with familiar products even in the face of major technology advances? Should they experiment with new offerings in hopes of attracting a more diverse customer group even at the risk of alienating their core supporters? These questions become more urgent as dot-coms spring up daily on the Web offering cheaper, faster, more personalized products and services that are attuned to the demands of the online environment.

Building on the PER effect allows companies to multiply their marketplace connections without sacrificing services to existing customers. The Web represents a breakthrough in corporate ability to sense new developments that are otherwise totally outside of the scope of market intelligence and analysis. The advantage of Internet-based companies and the digital value system framework is that they combine reach and online personalization with relationships across a much broader group of visitors and customers than the group traditional marketers can access. This broad group can be continually mined for information and trend analysis. This ability, combined with rapid reaction time and learn-by-doing skills, gives them a whole new range of relationships outside the scope of traditional companies and may well be the key to overcoming the innovator's dilemma.

Conclusion

It is no longer far-fetched to project the extension of the Internet into every company in the world and into the majority of households in industrialized countries. Instead of thinking of Internet users as a subset of their main customer base, managers have to gear up for business in a competitive environment where all their current customers are interconnected in various ways to the total subscriber base of the Net. For every company, no matter how large, the current customer base is only a small fraction of the overall marketplace. But it is the market at large, including that majority of "noncustomers," as Peter Drucker calls them, that is inevitably going to be the catalyst for far-ranging changes that will impact companies and their competitors. Drucker notes the following:

> Even the biggest enterprise (other than a government monopoly) has many more noncustomers than it has customers. There are very few institutions that supply as large a percentage of a market as 30 percent. There are therefore few institutions where the noncustomers do not amount to at least 70 percent of the potential market. And yet very few institutions know anything about the noncustomers—very few of them even know that they exist, let alone know who they are. And even fewer know why they are not customers. Yet it is with the noncustomers that changes always start.[7]

In an environment where product generations changed slowly and innovations took a long time to diffuse through to a level of mass adoption, having a marketplace blind spot was a vulnerability, but leading companies could devise strategies to pick up on changes and adapt their behavior and products accordingly. With the speed of development and diffusion today, this is not possible.

Exponential relationships build on constant interaction among all the participants in a digital value system. Companies track the online responses of current customers and broader market prospects to drive rapid improvements in services. They analyze and react quickly to a much broader span of information about the needs and interests of the entire market, representing both current and prospective customers. This gives them the ability to make a continual stream of changes and adjustments that are very much in synchronization with the growth cycles of technology and product demand instead of risking getting too far ahead or getting left behind as things move in totally new directions.

The Net makes relationships more complex, multidimensional, and volatile at the same time that it offers unprecedented opportunity to translate millions of online interactions into ties that will strengthen over time. Within a well-defined digital value system, these relationships are based on a rich vein of information and a solid foundation of trust. The change from batch-mode customer relationship management to real-time online responsiveness gives companies the chance to provide visible improvements with each new interaction. By moving through the stages of online relationship building, companies can enhance both the precision and the "stickiness" of interactions with online visitors in order to turn them into customers and keep them coming back.

Large technology companies are reinventing themselves as service providers to become more flexible in reaching and reacting to a diversified marketplace. Online service providers can track the needs of a broader base of customers for a wider set of solutions. In particular, vendors of expensive, high-end technology, such as Oracle databases, are experimenting with the ASP model. As previous chapters have suggested and as the next two chapters discuss, selling services associated with products is the preferred strategy for growth and profitability in the brokered economy that has developed on the Net. So it makes perfect sense that the smartest of the large companies are moving in this direction. As will always be the case in the Internet economy, however, they are finding that dot-coms are staking out the same territory, bringing the competition for customer relationships and service revenues to a new playing field.

C H A P T E R   S E V E N

From Commodity Products to Customized E-Services

Site traffic and stock valuations, portals and partnerships notwith-standing, at some point the Internet economy has to generate profits. Figuring out exactly where and how those profits will materialize is proving to be a formidable task for established companies and dot-coms alike. Managers have only recently come to terms with the Inter-net's proclivity to turn profitable products into freebies. Real-time financial information, in-depth news analysis, music, games—it seems that all the riches of the digital world are now delivered without charge to the desktop. And it's not just the bits that flow freely through the Internet economy. Personal computers—one of the growth indus-tries of the last century—are now the loss leaders that provide an incentive for customers to sign on for three years of low-priced Inter-net connectivity. Even the connectivity charge can be waived if the user agrees to look at Web advertisements for a few hours a day.

All these giveaways are supposed to be setting the stage for the next explosive round of online revenues. The bigger the investments, the higher the expectations for when the money finally does start to flow. But from where? Advertising certainly isn't going to put enough dollars into enough pockets to justify all the hype. Put together all the process efficiencies that the Web will generate in the manufacture and distribution of consumer goods over the next three years, and it still won't create enough profit margin on goods sold to meet revenue expectations for business-to-consumer dot-coms. It is no wonder, then, that more and more companies are focusing on providing Internet-based services to increase revenues. But these services are not automatically profitable, nor do they provide any guarantee against commoditization unless they are based on personal information, trust, and relationships. In other words, the most meaningful e-services will be part of a digital value system. This chapter analyzes how different types of companies are working to build such services.

The E-Service Imperative

Introducing a campaign to brand Hewlett-Packard as the leading e-services provider, CEO Carly Fiorina reflected a keen awareness that the move to e-services is important for everyone's bottom line: "[T]he challenge, for all of us, is to think about how to make money from e-services. Which e-services do you want to create, where do you want to deliver them, what eco-systems of services do you want to join, because e-services are built on communities of interests."[1] HP itself is betting the business on designing and delivering next-generation Internet-based services, but it is certainly not the only company to conclude that expanded online services holds the key to long-term growth and profitability in the Internet economy.

It makes perfect sense to focus on services as the profit center of the future. The Internet puts downward pricing pressure on tangible goods, turning many products into loss leaders and commodities. Easy access to online price comparisons and the aggregation of buyer power combine to challenge product differentiation and squeeze profit margins to the limit. Most traditional companies are already feeling the online pinch in some product line or pricing strategy, and the news is only going to get worse as business-to-business e-marketplaces proliferate over the next several years. The prospect of shoring up revenues with higher-margin and recurring service offerings has a built-in appeal. On the positive side of the ledger, the demand for services is also on the rise, as dot-coms that are focused on rapid growth count on service providers to accelerate projects and as established companies look to add flexibility by outsourcing peripheral functions. As long as the Internet continues to expand, this demand for services will grow along with it.

Services have fueled growth in the pre-Internet economy too, of course. For the past several decades, providing services has been a lot more profitable than manufacturing basic equipment, selling commodity products, or building infrastructure. A quick analysis of the profit profiles of Fortune 500 companies during the 1990s shows a clear trend: companies in the service sectors are growing faster, generating more shareholder value, and enjoying higher stock valuations. Hand in hand with the technology sector, service providers are poised to dominate the new century—but only if they can work out the economics of delivering more services more efficiently to more customers over the Internet.

But therein lies the rub. The drive to deliver online services is so widespread that it is easy to lose sight of the differences between simple service extensions from the bricks-and-mortar world and strategic new services with digital value. The pursuit of e-services simply to shore up the bottom line may well backfire if services themselves become commoditized in the transition to the Internet. The service focus within a digital value system is to generate increasing value for the customer as well as the service provider. By developing services that are based on information, trust, and relationships, companies will create a self-sustaining source of revenue at a diminishing cost.

Defining E-Services

There are multiple incentives, including cost savings, reaching new markets, and just answering customer demand, for companies to move existing services online. But a simple transfer of today's services to the Internet does not generate significant new value even though it might offer convenience and cost savings for all parties. Ordering a pizza for home delivery on the Internet instead of on the phone does not qualify as a new type of e-service. Providing services for an Internet-connected kitchen network that allows subscribers to turn on the oven or the microwave and cook the pizza before they get home definitely does. A defining characteristic of e-services is that they change the status quo by leveraging the capabilities of the Internet to accomplish something that was previously impossible or they transform the economics of a service to make it available to a different market or at a significantly lower price. Additional e-service components include the ability to deliver and support the service via the Internet and the possibility of rapidly increasing the service capacity to expand as needed in response to customer demand. Sustainable e-services will also generate visible value for the customer and can be highly customized by the individual to create loyalty and avoid commoditization.

Within this context, managers face many choices in designing and implementing an e-services strategy, and some decisions are more Net-centric and value-laden than others. It is important to analyze the different types of services that are emerging from the Internet today and to understand how these fit within a digital value system. In the face of competition and rapid obsolescence, providing customized e-services leverages the relationships and trust that are already in place and builds increasing value into an expanding customer and partnership base.

Obviously, companies that can move seamlessly from a product base to an e-services strategy are in the best position to maximize the opportunities of the networked marketplace. They are able to connect customers to a cornucopia of related products and services. Bundling of interconnected services reduces the move toward comparison shopping because full service solutions are not as easy to pick apart and compare on the basis of price alone. The more that customers take advantage of high-value services, the more they benefit, the more trust and reliance they place on the providers of the services, and the more information they feed back into the system to guide providers in building in even more value to the next generation. But this added value has to be seen and felt by customers to keep this cycle moving in a positive direction.

E-Services and the Economics of Digital Value

In chapter 3 we discussed the new economy's emerging ability to transform a one-shot product sale, even of a commodity, into a cascade of follow-on product and services offerings based on the original sale. It was already clear that the toaster services were going to generate far more value for all parties over the life of the toaster than its initial sale. Keeping close to the customer and providing those services was a prize worth reaching for and capturing.

In chapters 4 through 6 we traced the transformation of a one-time information collection event into a long-term trust-based relationship, occurring within the digital value system. This transformation started with a solitary customer interaction—a product purchase or a Web site registration—which the company nurtured and grew into an on-going sequence of ever richer and ever more efficient business-and-customer interactions.

Some of the important economic benefits of this progression are illustrated in figure 7-1, which, among other things, shows the reduction of customer retention costs through a continuous e-services focus. Because of the ongoing and integrated nature of a digital value relationship, the cost of each additional sale (the acquisition cost) effectively goes to zero for e-service customers, while the probability that each additional information-driven, customer-tailored offer is accepted goes to one.

Because of the trust growing within the relationship, the cost of maintaining this relationship—the customer retention cost—also

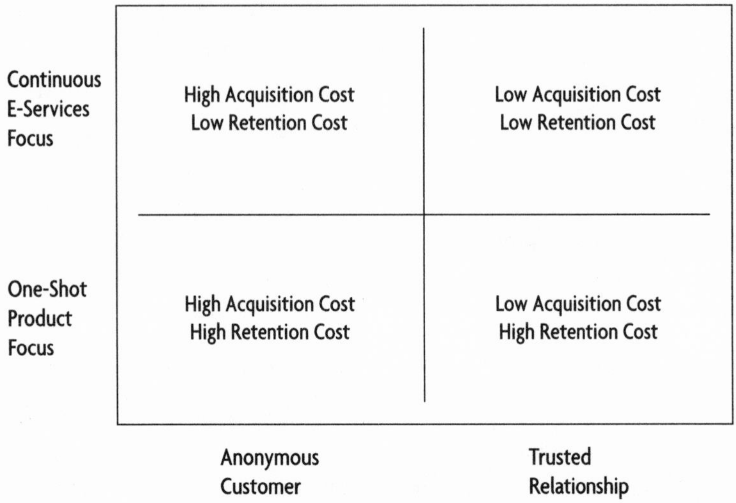

	Anonymous	Trusted
Continuous E-Services Focus	High Acquisition Cost Low Retention Cost	Low Acquisition Cost Low Retention Cost
One-Shot Product Focus	High Acquisition Cost High Retention Cost	Low Acquisition Cost High Retention Cost

Anonymous Customer	Trusted Relationship

Figure 7-1 Customer Costs as a Function of Relationship Type

tends to zero. In a sense the relationship reaches a self-sustaining state in which both the business and the customer derive continual value and efficiency and work together to design new service offerings. This desirable state of affairs contrasts with the estimated cost of converting a new Web site visitor into a buyer in the first place, pegged at $40 per customer for leading retail Web sites by a study conducted by the Boston Consulting Group and shop.org.[2] Unless Web merchants do manage to turn a healthy percentage of these first-time buyers into high-value e-service customers, their cost of doing business will spiral out of control.

The company with processes that are informed and driven by a carefully elucidated digital value system will be able to reduce customer acquisition and retention costs and extend the benefits of the lifetime customer relationship by offering continuous e-service options. In the Internet economy, the cost of sales and the cost of customer retention are the effective measures of e-service success.

The closer these figures are to zero, the better the firm's long-term prospects.

Intuit's e-services strategy provides a real-world example of the digital value cycle in operation. Intuit is using the Internet to leverage its strong market lead in accounting software for small business owners by offering new services to its primary small business customers. In the process it is forging new partnerships with companies that also want to provide services to this highly attractive market. More than 2 million business owners already use QuickBooks to manage their finances. Once these small companies have learned the QuickBooks system and have input all their financial data into the program, they have moved into a trusted relationship with Quicken and have wittingly or not established fairly high switching costs. Orphaning their financial records and learning another system becomes less and less likely as the small businesses input still further information and connect their QuickBooks data to other systems. In fact, QuickBooks customers are remarkably if at times grudgingly loyal.

The QuickBooks customer pool is a prime target for extended business services from Intuit itself and from its business partners. In 1999 Intuit seized this opportunity by launching the QuickBooks Internet Gateway service for its small business customers and simultaneously announcing that nine business partners had signed on to deliver integrated services through the Gateway ranging from electronic stamps and desktop mailing to online loans and backup storage facilities.

Everyone stands to benefit from this expanded service orbit. The small business owners who are already QuickBooks customers get free access to the basic services of the Quickbooks Internet Gateway and pay as needed for one or more of the advanced services. Some of the partner companies offer free initial trials or other incentives to motivate adoption of their products. Because each partner's service has been pre-integrated with QuickBooks, users get the added advantage of largely trouble-free implementation and few barriers to adoption.

That helps to overcome some of the biggest hurdles in selling to small companies, the inherent resistance of small business owners to bring new and untested technology into the company and the lack of time to learn and integrate new systems. According to Intuit:

> The QuickBooks Internet Gateway solves two problems facing business-to-business e-service and e-commerce firms. Firstly, it's a channel, enabling B2B firms to acquire customers from QuickBook's base of more than two million small businesses. Secondly, it is a platform enabling B2B firms to integrate technically their services into Quick-Books. QuickBooks customers' use of technology is likely to result in significant customer acquisition and rapid adoption of the B2B e-services. On average, QuickBooks customers spend more than 10 hours a week using QuickBooks software to manage their businesses.[3]

In exchange for providing its own customers with enhanced services and its partners with a direct channel for new customer acquisition, Intuit has already received commitments for close to $70 million in placement fees and revenue sharing. That's a considerable new source of revenues, but it is only the beginning of the value for Intuit and for the participating e-service providers. Through this new online connection to small business owners, Intuit and its Gateway partners are in the best position to find out more about the needs of small business owners as they begin to take the Internet more seriously. Within this digital value system, the upside for all participants is unlimited. Business owners get more services that can be more easily implemented, Gateway partners get access and ongoing connections to millions of high-value customers, and Intuit has even more incentives for its existing customers to stick with Quick-Books and a more attractive offer for potential customers. Plus, as the center of this particular digital system, Intuit gets an increasing share of the all action in terms of direct revenues and indirect information and relationship value.

Putting Services Inside

Not every service offer meets the criteria of increasing digital value for all participants as clearly as the Intuit program. Companies have taken a number of different approaches to rolling out e-services, depending on their core business and the needs of customers and partners. Intel chairman Andy Grove's frequently cited assertion that every company has to become an Internet company in order to survive, needs updating now that the Internet economy has taken hold. Today, it appears that every company needs to offer some form of e-services in order to be profitable.

Intel itself has joined the rush to e-services with flashy marketing messages on its consumer-oriented Web pages and a more serious business-to-business bid to become a worldwide leader in e-commerce application services and Web hosting. The Intel services aimed at individual users promise excitement at the cutting edge of technology, signing on consumers who want to keep up with the latest and greatest online experiences—or as the online marketing message puts it, "What you can't do in life, you can do on the Web." Despite all the enhanced graphics of the Intel consumer site, what you can't do in real life boils down to a pretty basic list of multimedia activities: downloading and mixing digital music, creating and exchanging digital photographs and images, playing online games and media-enhanced shopping sprees. The service component is limited to third-party demonstration software that users can download on their own machines. In exchange, they will be getting additional offers from the companies that designed it. To Intel's credit, this trade-off is clearly spelled out on the site, and the exchange of value is reasonable. Intel and partners benefit from information about the interests and the tool selection of early adopters, and the user gets a well-organized, free download site and some good tips on applications.

A more serious strategic move to services as a line of business is Intel's heavily marketed Internet hosting and application services. Clearly aimed at capturing a share of the international e-business boom, these services are designed for active e-commerce practitioners and large corporations that want to outsource their critical operations. Intel will offer public Web hosting and order-processing servers along with the software applications that are needed to keep Web services running at peak performance. At first glance, it might be hard to see how this move fits into Intel's prowess in chip production. Unlike IBM, an e-business pioneer and still a leader in turning hardware experience into consulting and other services, Intel doesn't have a relevant background in facilities management, computer center operations, or large-scale software application hosting. Nonetheless, it is making a strong case for leveraging its success in internal Internet and online sales (more than $1 billion monthly from the public Intel Web site) along with its reputation for quality and its dominance of one area of the technology marketplace.

To make up for its late start in services, Intel plans to invest more than a billion dollars in building up a network of at least twelve worldwide facilities. This will just put it into the same competitive field as established application hosting providers such as Exodus and AT&T. But clearly Intel is positioning itself for the long run, looking to diversify from its position at the headwaters of hardware and component manufacturing to become an end-to-end provider of digital value.

In fact, it is hard to find a company that is taking the Internet seriously and is not busy reinventing itself as a service provider of some sort. Despite the crowd of e-service converts, there are some clear patterns that can be used to sort out and evaluate different service strategies. We will take a look at the different ways that companies are moving toward e-services, from a path that is clearly grounded in manufacturing and retail business models to technology-driven forays into serving a future that is still unfolding. At one end of the spectrum are automotive manufacturers and supermarket chains that are still battling structural industry restraints. At the other are technology and telecommunications companies that have already survived one round of online convergence and are gearing up for the next.

All of these models for service design and delivery will continue to evolve and expand based on customer reception. In fact, the hallmark of any successful digital service provider will be the ability to keep ahead of the curve by offering innovation and discovery blended in with well-accepted service modules. Since there are many service providers and only limited attention and loyalty from business and consumers, being first out of the gate with a high-value digital service offer and then following it up with a cluster of related services is going to be a major advantage. If the early mover can leverage the experience and information from a full-fledged digital value relationship with the customer, there may never be a motivation for switching to another service provider. This is the closest any online company can hope to get to winning the loyalty of a customer for life. So no matter where companies start along the path to implementing e-services, it is in their interest to keep moving and as quickly as possible.

Bridges from the Bricks-and-Mortar World

For companies anchored to a traditional set of products and a channel-constrained industry structure, the lure of e-services is especially compelling. Internet competitors are everywhere, profit margins are eroding, and markets for existing products and services are fully mature. Examples from three such industries—groceries, semiconductors, and automotive—illustrate that even entrenched companies can use their online experience and Internet programs in one area to build bridges from current business models to more flexible e-service opportunities.

Tesco

In the grocery industry, established supermarket chains are confronting a combination of online threats and incentives. Storefronts face stiff competition from Web grocery services that provide comparable prices and the added value of free delivery. Many of the Web-based supermarkets are already creating their own value-added services, expanding to include dry cleaning, video rental, and restaurant deliveries to become a total home delivery and convenience provider.

Despite the spread of loyalty programs and branded discount cards, the typical grocery chain provides very few consumer incentives for in-person shopping. All of these trends mean that grocery chains are particularly vulnerable to the threat of online competition. But the stores can also use their existing customer base and the reach of the Net to expand into higher-value services. If they embrace the e-services concept, incumbents have some key advantages in terms of regional points of presence, inventory and logistics management experience, and economies of scale.

The U.K.-based supermarket chain Tesco demonstrates how the Internet can support a move from commodity product to a cluster of higher-margin services. Tesco has leveraged customer relationships created in the bricks-and-mortar world by extending its service offerings into other domains with more virtual value potential, such as insurance and financial services.

Tesco started to expand its trust relationship with customers in the supermarket world with a loyalty card offer that provided the typical checkout discounts and special deals for frequent shoppers. Tesco followed on with some basic financial services that took advantage of this capability to make life easier for customers. Customers could cash paychecks and deposit funds in Tesco savings and checking accounts. The response to this service was overwhelmingly positive, providing a green light to the introduction of broader services over the Internet. Within a year Tesco expanded its range of online services far beyond order and delivery of household items and groceries. Now the company offers insurance of all types, including pet insurance, via its Web site. In fact, Tesco has leveraged the Net to become a major U.K. insurance distributor.

In addition, Tesco now offers loans and credit services and pension funds, as well as general online banking and branded credit cards and even automotive services. In addition to its online grocery services it now sells books, gifts, and electronics items on the Internet. The company is also testing a new program that gives bar code readers to customers to attach to their PalmPilots or other personal digital assistants (PDAs) in order to use at home for scanning in and automatically ordering items that they want delivered.

To broaden its customer relationship base even further, Tesco also offers free Internet access to any of its customers. In making its move from product company to service provider, Tesco focused on cross-selling to existing customers first, then expanding its offers to a broader online market. This allowed it to roll out increasingly sophisticated Internet services in manageable stages and build the feedback from early adopters into later versions. While Tesco intends to maintain its bricks-and-mortar outlets, it has successfully diversified its revenue base by adding a number of high-margin services and attracting new types of customers. This lays the foundation for the next cycle of service expansion and the design of advanced e-services.

National Semiconductor

National Semiconductor has been working for the past several years to accomplish a similar feat of revenue diversification, and delivering services via the Internet has been an important part of its efforts. Even though this multinational manufacturer of semiconductors and other electronic components employs an extensive direct sales force and multiple distribution channels, it has put special emphasis on serving its primary customer—the design engineer—through its Web site. Like many companies, National Semiconductor aims to gain customer loyalty and increase sales revenues by making the Web site an information-rich channel for its products with hundreds of thousands of pages of product specifications. E-commerce capabilities have made it easy for end users to order small quantities of products, and customized extranet access has aided purchasing agents with more traditional business-to-business needs.

Based on the trust it has established with distributors and other partners, National has also been active in information pooling—putting together all the distributors and vendors onto a single, customizable page that includes individual order history. This allows customers to check on inventory status and make direct orders from their vendor of choice. All of these features have made the National Web site a magnet for design engineers around the world, drawing hundreds of thousands of unique visits and interactions every month. In the process of responding to its end users and collecting information about their needs, National has also learned to anticipate demand for its products in the marketplace. However important these benefits may be to National and to its users, they have not added new sources of revenue. Joining the migration to e-services is part of a strategic shift to new products and services to improve National Semiconductor's bottom line.

One small step in this direction is selling real-time workbench simulation and testing services over the Web in order to simplify the laboratory testing work of the engineers. National is partnering with Transim, a simulation software company based in Seattle, to roll out its online services. The first customer group is specialists in electronic components involving power supply. One of the tasks of these engineers is determining how well a specific component will work at different input power levels, a job that can take weeks to complete in a typical laboratory environment, but takes just a few hours on the Power.national.com Web site using a new online service called WebSim.

According to Phil Gibson, director of interactive services for National Semiconductor's online service initiative, WebSim and the Power.national.com site are the first manifestations of a strategic migration toward e-services for the company as a whole:

> Power.national.com is the first roll out but we expect that this will grow to include a portal for other focused sectors over time. We see affiliate revenue opportunities in listing all the other components from other sites, and the growth potential to make services a large part of our program over time.[4]

National is not measuring the success of WebSim solely in terms of the immediate revenues it generates. In the long term, National is counting on such projects to refine its own understanding of the overall e-services market and to build its reputation as a high-value source of online services among its end users. That in turn will support more ambitious e-services programs in the future.

Ford

In the automotive industry, the leading carmakers are working over-time to stake out their own e-services territory in the face of resistance from bricks-and-mortar dealerships and competition for consumer loyalty from Web-based auto-shopping services. The dealerships are wedded to their current sales models and are blocking the automak-ers from selling directly to the public. Meanwhile, online auto sites are becoming more aggressive about providing value-added services rather than simply referring visitors to the closest dealership. Who-ever can capture consumer trust and create incentives for information sharing about vehicle performance or car loans will be well posi-tioned to become a key service provider for any number of adjunct products and services. That ultimate prize motivated Ford's man-agement to put e-services on a fast track.

One concrete move into the follow-on services business came when Ford acquired the Kwik-Fit chain of British car service centers in 1999. With more than 1,900 service points around the U.K., Kwik-Fit gave Ford an extensive window on the after-sale experience of the car-buying public. The automaker followed up later that year by pur-chasing a Florida-based "used parts recycling company," less euphe-mistically called a junkyard, with the intention of launching a used parts business on the Internet. Analysts were not quite sure what to make of the move, but Ford CEO Jacques Nasser insisted that it was another facet of the overall strategy of expanding Ford's footprint in Net-based services. By launching a global used parts Web site, Ford aimed to establish closer connections with the body shops, service centers, and insurance companies.

But the connection that has so far proved elusive for Ford, and every other auto manufacturer, is a direct online sales link to consumers. Ford's answer to the consumer connection challenge is an alliance with Microsoft's CarPoint Web site. This alliance allows prospective buyers to order various models of Fords on the Web, configuring the vehicles to suit their personal tastes. CarPoint will still bring a dealer into the negotiation, as required by current franchise laws, to make the actual pricing and delivery commitment. But at least the site now bears the Ford brand and captures extremely valuable information about consumer tastes and interests. Although no one is willing to comment on long-term plans to eliminate dealers' involvement, it is clear that Ford is just a short step away from direct online sales once the dealership franchise barriers are removed. If and when this happens, Ford will be ready to provide automotive e-services from online selection of a new car to the final disposal of surplus parts in an online junkyard. Ford will participate in the lifetime revenue stream of the automobile, from the assembly line to Sandy's Salvage Yard. But they will find themselves in a fierce competition for customers.

The Attractions of E-Application Services

Instead of using its direct sales force to sell its software at prices as high as half a million dollars, Oracle has followed the lead of Cisco Systems and has decided to rely on the Web as a sales channel for all but its multimillion-dollar negotiated contracts. It has also slashed software prices. CEO Larry Ellison asserts that the drastic price cuts were aimed at making Oracle products more appealing and accessible to the legions of small companies that are climbing on board the e-commerce bandwagon and finding themselves in need of more serious database management tools. These fast-growing companies don't have the budget to buy the high-priced Oracle solutions, even though they are struggling to manage growing mounds of data. But price is not the only barrier. Smaller companies seldom have the in-house technical expertise or the hardware to implement an Oracle-style solution. Price cuts, therefore, are just one component of Oracle's new strategies. The other initiative is a move to provide Oracle capabilities in the form of application services. Now companies of all sizes will be able to sign on for as many slices of Oracle database management software as they need for particular applications. This opens up a whole new market sector for Oracle.

Much of the interaction with smaller customers will take place on the Web or through certified ASP (application service provider) distribution partners, saving on the expense of sales calls and direct pitches. The added efficiency will help to increase Oracle's margin on the lower-priced software, and the application services business will provide a whole new revenue stream. Most important, the move puts Oracle squarely into the service business.

Almost every company today has easy access to the technology that is needed to become an ASP and adopting this model for service delivery means that they can build a revenue stream around a particular area of expertise—even one that is a lot narrower than Oracle's or National Semiconductor's. Take this development to its logical conclusion, and you have what are now called "syndication services," small services that are distributed in real-time and used over and over again for a small fee. As described by *Red Herring*, these fine-grained services are likely to pop up all over the Internet:

> Application syndication is like a giant Mixmaster, stirring and pulling sites apart into their constituent components. With application syndication, a business can give its suppliers, partners, distributors, and customers direct access to its inventory systems, catalog, sales data, and more—without going through expensive and time-consuming supply-chain integration efforts.[5]

Companies will soon be in a position to sell slices of services via the Web for only pennies per use. At first glance this seems like the irresistible opportunity every company is hoping for to capitalize on the revenue upside of services. If only they can generate an option that is in demand over and over again for a small fee, the revenue will mushroom as their applet spreads around the Net.

But the capability to slice and dice and respond on cue to the immediate demands of a large number of users does not necessarily mean that there is parallel potential for increasing value and personalization. Managers have to stay in close touch with what the user wants to accomplish and where they are heading next. Otherwise the syndicated service model is likely to generate interchangeable generic offerings that can be replaced all too easily with a more fully featured service slice.

Hewlett-Packard is facing this dilemma in its own e-services strategy. On the one hand, it would like to see a groundswell of demand for e-services everywhere. CEO Carly Fiorina describes the potential of building the Web into every possible appliance and generating services as a great opportunity:

> Everything with a microchip in it can become connected to the Web and so appliances will be all kinds of things. Things we've not thought of as information appliances will become them and these appliances, these devices will be large, and they'll be very small. They can be as large as a mega-videotron in a football stadium. Or, if HP researchers have their way, they can be as small as a few molecules thick. Think about what we could do with a device connected to the Web that was just a few molecules thick.[6]

HP's premise that reinventing itself around providing e-services makes perfect sense as a corporate branding strategy. Staking out a broad claim to e-services projects will help to ensure that HP is closely identified with at least some of the transformational business models that are bound to emerge in this area over the next several years. But talking about pervasive services and even creating prototypes and pilot projects are not the same as launching viable service offerings. Even the coolest of these ideas won't have a strategic impact until the company starts to roll out e-services that touch the lives of millions of Internet users. When this happens, HP will be in the position of letting its services speak for themselves.

Conclusion

There may be no limit to the number of specialized services that can be spun off the Web, but not all of these services are going to be worth enough to subscribe to them, much less pay for them. There are several major categories of e-services offered today:

- personalized services that enable users to get more out of the products and interactions that they are already familiar with;
- new services introduced to leverage existing relationships and digital delivery options; and
- totally new categories of services that are especially suited to Internet development and delivery.

Established companies who know their customers and are able to package value in attractive bundles of services and products are the major players in the first e-services category. Part of a winning digital value strategy will be having the critical service pieces for your most important customer groups and being in a position to predict which services they are going to want now and tomorrow. The best way to accomplish that is honing your information and trust and relationship strategies first, then using them to define and create the right package of services.

The more options they must chose from and the more complex their lives and work become, the more customers will be looking for simplification and integration from their e-service providers. Customers don't want randomized services any more than they want random chunks of information from an Internet connection. Companies may choose to be their own integrators, but it is likely that the rise of e-services will create yet another service category—the service integrator. This desire for integrated services will be to the advantage of the multifunctional service providers that have created successful digital value systems. These companies are already in a position to package services according to a variety of tastes and to charge differential rates for each bundle to maximize the value/revenue relationship with the individual customer.

In all of this information-rich and trust-driven mixing and matching, it is crucial for individual companies to keep a firm grasp on the shared-value payoff that fully developed e-services provide for customers. They need to provide a distinctive service based on a trusted relationship to retain existing customers. Customers receiving such personalized attention are much less likely to make purchase decisions based solely on price—a constant danger of the brokered economy. We will take a closer look at the impact of the brokered economy on relationships and services in chapter 8.

CHAPTER EIGHT

Inside the Brokered Economy

The prospect of dynamic pricing spreading like wildfire across all industries and product categories represents a change so vast in its implications that skepticism is a natural first reaction. A long list of barriers and caveats springs immediately to mind—too complicated, too disruptive, not appropriate for most products, and so on. Pricing strategy is one of the most challenging areas for management—both mistakes and breakthroughs are glaringly apparent on the bottom line. The last thing a well-established and successful company wants to do is throw out its carefully crafted pricing policies and jump into the midst of an unpredictable global electronic auction pit. The complexities of dynamic online pricing suddenly make the challenge of channel conflict look like a piece of cake.

But what if the choice really does come down to embracing dynamic pricing or losing prime customers to auction-enabled competitors? An objective analysis of current trends and the intrinsic capabilities of the Net argues that this may well be the scenario for large and small companies sooner than most managers can imagine it.

Conviction about the inevitable triumph of dynamic pricing—the fluctuation of prices according to demand—on the Internet comes naturally to Kip Frey. After all, he is president of an e-commerce enterprise that depends on the proliferation of online auctions for its own survival. Specifically, OpenSite sells its auction management software and systems to hundreds of companies that have incorporated online bidding into their business models. Headquartered in Durham, North Carolina, OpenSite now claims more than 50 percent of the Internet auction software market for companies that opt to buy a commercial auction package rather than build it themselves in-house. As dynamic pricing applications take hold around the Internet, selling the tools that enable companies to put their products up for bid is a hot growth area.

But Frey's insistence on the inexorable spread of dynamic pricing on the Internet is not based solely on the fortunes of his company. He grounds his argument in the historical context of price-setting practice, pointing out that the current reliance on fixed prices is a relatively recent phenomenon. What's more, he asserts the following:

> Static pricing simply cannot survive on the Internet. Today's market leaders rely on exploiting numerous blind spots and inefficiencies in the marketplace when they set their prices. That's something they just can't get away with in a vastly more efficient electronic exchange that generates comparative information in real time. I envision a world in which dynamic pricing is an everyday part of life for businesses and consumers. If today's leading companies don't embrace this concept, they will die.[1]

Other auction software providers, perhaps worried about scaring away prospective customers with too much talk about economic upheaval, tend to position their products as more of a complement than a threat to the traditional system. In fact, Anne Perlman, president and CEO of Moai Technologies, a rival of OpenSite's auction technology, takes the opposite tack from Frey and tries to assuage fears about the disruptive potential of online auctions by focusing on Moai's role as another sales channel. Perlman suggests the following:

> Mostly, it'll be augmenting it [existing sales channels]. So,
> for example, in the use of auctions for either excess or aging
> inventory, frequently what it's doing is augmenting a sales
> force that used to call or fax brokers and sell the inventory
> to them through the broker channel. Now with auctions,
> instead of selling to brokers, they might sell to resellers or
> distributors. So that's an augmentation, really, of the old
> style…if you will, conventional style of doing business. So
> that's probably the main way that it will be done.[2]

Offering reassurance to late adopters instead of predicting their
demise may be a more effective marketing tactic, but Frey's more radical
position does have strong third-party opinion behind it. Forrester
Research predicts that overall business-to-business transactions over the
Internet will account for $2.7 trillion in trade by 2004 and that 53 percent
of this amount will be handled by e-marketplaces.[3] The same report
asserts that by 2002, 93 percent of all large companies expect to do some
of their buying and selling using e-marketplaces. Since e-marketplace is
the general term for all Internet-based trading venues, the transactions
predicted by Forrester will not necessarily involve dynamic pricing. But
most e-marketplaces will have an auction component that is expected to
increase in popularity over the next several years.

Web-based auctions are no longer a novelty. As the original super-
star of online consumer auctions, eBay set out in 1996 to demonstrate
that the Internet is uniquely suited to connecting millions of potential buyers with millions of entrepreneurial sellers and that hosting
that point of connection is indeed a major business opportunity.
Three million customers and $700 million in revenues later, eBay is
still going strong. The tidal wave of traffic and transactions on eBay
has spawned competitors and imitators from Amazon and Yahoo! to
thousands of more narrowly focused Web sites that have sprung up to
offer markets for all types of consumer goods and services. But these
consumer-dominated bidding fests don't seem to have much to do
with the trillion-dollar pricing and distribution systems of business-
to-business exchanges predicted by Forrester. And most of today's

auction sites don't seem to pose the dire threat to old economy survival that Frey implies is intrinsic in the spread of online dynamic pricing. Nor, at first glance, do OpenSite's current customers look much like the advance shock troops of a serious threat to the pricing policies of well-established multinational corporations.

OpenSite-enabled companies are certainly using the auction mode to sell products—exclusively or as a supplement to existing pricing structures. One customer site, for example, Artnet.com, serves as a portal to the world of art for dealers, collectors, artists, and enthusiasts, and claims that it is revolutionizing the art market with the only continuous online fine art auctions featuring works by blue-chip artists. To attract traffic to its site, Artnet.com also provides access to 2 million auction price records from more than 500 auction houses worldwide.

In another field altogether, Dexpo gives the dental community an easy and effective way to shop for and order dental supplies and equipment. The Dexpo site continually hosts different sales and auctions representing products from the entire dental community in an attempt to attract as many bidders as possible in a fairly small overall market. Another business-to-business auction sponsor, ecFood.com, provides an online commercial exchange for food-related companies to trade everything from food and packaging to equipment items in a secure and private environment. E-fibre.com plays a similar role for the paper industry. Claiming pioneering status as the Internet's first live auction site to sell pulp and papermaking fibers, E-fibre.com offers buyers and sellers of pulp and papermaking products ensured quality by also acting as a quality intermediary. In its neutral party role, the site provides grade definitions, manufacturing region information, and other quality control measures to ensure customer satisfaction.

A mix of business and consumer customers can take advantage of the Salvage Direct Web site, which allows insurance companies and financial institutions to auction reclaimed vehicles. Bidders find deals on all types of vehicles from Harleys and SUVs to snowmobiles and trucks that have been recovered from thefts, have been repossessed by banks, or need to be rebuilt because of accident damage. Salvage Direct also allows dealers and other individuals to auction complete vehicles, parts, and other automotive-related goods, such as tools, on its site.

Granted, these are interesting applications of dynamic pricing in a variety of industries, but even thousands of such sites would not add up to a major revolution in pricing and product distribution strategies. If this customer group represented the future face of online dynamic pricing, then the average Fortune 500 company would not be likely to feel much heat. It is not any particular online auction site that threatens established pricing and value models, but that potent Internet combination of information pooling and open global access. This searchlight exposes the inefficiencies in today's prevailing price structures and gives motivated buyers easy access to a greatly expanded set of alternative suppliers. Fixed pricing depends on limited information on the buyer side and fewer opportunities on the supplier side. The result has been information gaps—dark corners in the marketplace that were too out of the way to illuminate before. Now the Internet has come along to cast a giant spotlight into every nook and cranny. As market inefficiencies are exposed, buyers have greater motivation to seek out more favorable pricing and the information ammunition to strike a harder bargain.

This chapter will analyze the forces that are driving the spread of dynamic pricing on the Internet and discuss the potential impact on every type of company. A roadmap for the evolution of the brokered economy will show that the dynamic pricing phenomenon has the potential to be either disruptive or complementary, depending on its application to different types of markets.

Roadmap for the Brokered Economy

In terms of sizing the auction component of e-marketplaces, industry analysts project a variety of different growth numbers and trajectories, but they seem united in predicting rapid expansion of dynamic pricing on the Internet over the next several years. Gartner Group, for example, expects to see the formation of between 7,500 and 10,000 completely new Net markets established by 2002. It predicts that these will cover all the basic industry groups and reach into very specific niche product sales between businesses.

An even more aggressive projection comes from Vernon Keenan, Internet analyst at Keenan Vision, who estimates that about $3.8 billion in transactions, or 10 percent of all Internet commerce, took place via online auction in 1998. Keenan asserts that approximately 39 percent of business-to-business Internet commerce will be conducted using dynamic pricing mechanisms by 2004, that overall business-to-business Internet commerce will reach $1.1 trillion in the United States by the date, and that $439 billion of that would be derived from dynamic pricing transactions.

Keenan backs up his high numbers with the observation that Microsoft entered the auction tools market in 1998. He sees this as providing an enormous boost to the business-to-business auction trend because now every company that uses the Microsoft server will have easy and free access to the key auction enabler technology:

"Microsoft just added a free Auction component for its SiteServer 3.0 Commerce Edition. Microsoft's entry into the auction software marketplace will change the dynamics of the industry and accelerate the use of auction technology, aiding the growth of the Internet Exchange."[4]

As we will see later in the chapter, a spate of high-priced acquisitions of business-to-business auction enablers adds even more credence to the high-end estimate of how fast the online brokered economy is likely to grow. Before discussing the impact on specific companies in any detail, it is useful to define the different types of auctions that are common in today's online market and to discuss how the introduction of online auctions and differential pricing on the whole is likely to impact different market segments.

Table 8-1 lists the three most common auction types. When thinking of auctions, most people automatically picture an English auction, in which the highest bid wins. This is a straightforward and well-understood model, and it makes perfect sense for eBay and other consumer-oriented auctions on the Web. This model also tends to garner

AUCTION TYPE	CHARACTERISTICS
English, or Ascending-price	This is the most familiar type of consumer auction. The seller announces an opening bid price and bidding gets progressively higher until it reaches the level where demand tapers off. When no additional bids are made, the auction is over, and the final highest bidder is declared the winner. (The Yankee auction is a variant of the English auction.)
Dutch, or Descending-price	The seller announces a very high opening bid. Bids are lowered progressively until the demand rises to match supply. This type is useful for auctioning multiple lots of identical quality.
First-price, or Sealed Bid	Bids are typically by invitation only. They are submitted in written form based on specifications about the product or project but with no knowledge of the bids of others. The winner pays the exact amount of the bid. This type is often used to award contracts.

Table 8-1 The Three Most Common Internet Auction Types

the highest return for the seller, whose participation is of prime importance in maintaining liquidity for online auctions. The Dutch auction has been adopted by W. R. Hambrecht & Co. as a new way to price company shares in IPOs. This application will be discussed in greater detail in the final section of this chapter. The first-price, or sealed bid, model is most common on Web sites that manage business-to-business vendor and supplier bids. The more comprehensive dynamic pricing environments that are emerging for entire industries tend to offer all of these options, depending on the type of goods to be sold, in order to provide maximum flexibility for buyers and sellers.

Understanding the type of auctions that are most common on the Internet is helpful, but much more important is developing a sense for how disruptive the different iterations of dynamic pricing are likely to be. Will the rise of dynamic pricing spell trouble for companies that refuse to participate, or will auction sales fold gracefully into existing business models? Figure 8-1 maps out the impact of auctions in different industry situations, from the least likely to cause industry-wide disruption to the most disruptive.

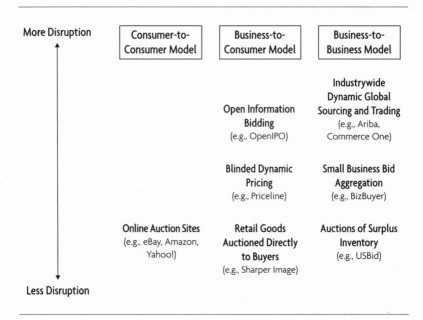

Figure 8-1 Potential Disruptive Impact of Dynamic Pricing Models

Consumer-to-Consumer Auctions

Even though eBay and other consumer auction sites have captured the lion's share of media attention and the popular imagination, moving consumer-to-consumer exchange onto the Web is not intrinsically disruptive, as anyone who has been to a flea market or a garage sale can attest. Though some new goods are traded on eBay, and some businesses participate, the bulk of goods on offer at any given time have already been in circulation. As much as eBay has been a boon to collectors and secondhand aficionados, and notwithstanding the fact that it now generates considerable income for full-time "power sellers," the auctioning of used goods remains more of a substitute for secondhand shops than a major threat to established businesses. Which is not to say that eBay does not have enormous influence on the acceptance of auction models or a major economic impact within its own digital value system. To the extent that successful eBay merchants now make their living from activity on the site or have been inspired to branch out into ventures of their own, eBay has contributed mightily to the overall growth of the Internet economy. Consumers are also introduced to the notion that prices are not carved in stone. But this has mainly taken the form of substitution instead of disruption. The same is true for the other general and specialized consumer auction sites.

The dynamic pricing for new, branded consumer goods that is taking place on buyer aggregation sites such as Mercata is based on volume discount rather than direct bidding. Customers register to buy an item at a stated price, but the price goes down as more buyers sign on. Buyer aggregation sites do not account for nearly as many transactions as auctions at this point, but in the long run this model does have potential to disrupt fixed-price, retail sales. Even though the goods in the buyer aggregation model flow from business to consumer, the key relationships are those among the consumers themselves. Once the average consumer gets a sense that every purchase can be negotiated simply by registering at a Web site and waiting for the price to drop, there will be strong pressure on retailers to offer some kind of dynamic price scale. Most of these consumer aggregation sites were launched in 1999, so their popularity and actual impact on prices won't be clear for a while. But the model of buyer aggregation, combined with the massive reach of the Internet and the increasing acceptance of online shopping make this category one to watch in terms of longer term disruptive impact.

Business-to-Consumer Auctions

As is the case in the consumer-to-consumer segment, the fact that traditional retail stores are putting new goods up for auction does not mean that core business models are threatened. The Sharper Image and other popular brand Web sites are taking advantage of strong traffic flow to very selectively distribute surplus inventory directly to customers on the Net. But these same items would have gone to offline discounters in any case, and the bulk of such goods still do.

Adding an auction component to their sites gives retailers a chance to experiment in a low-risk, low-profile way with consumer-oriented dynamic pricing, but it does not imply any immediate intention to abandon traditional retail models.

The disruptive impact of Priceline, which started out by letting consumers bid for airline tickets and other time-sensitive items, could be considerable. The "name-your-own-price" company now offers consumers dynamic pricing on grocery shopping and car rentals, cars and interest rates, with other items waiting in the wings. The brisk trade in Priceline-brokered airline tickets indicates that many consumers have been won over to the Priceline model despite some issues with its low fulfillment rates. In order to become a truly disruptive force, however, Priceline would have to provide more of an information-pooling service for its customers. Now customers are deliberately cut off from participating in or learning from the process that goes on behind the scenes as Priceline staff negotiate with the airlines.

As we saw in chapter 4, release of process information to the marketplace is a key factor in empowering the buyer and creating an incentive for action. With its current model, Priceline keeps hold of all the information about market dynamics, and consumers are no wiser (and only occasionally richer) than they would be from dealing with a traditional fare discounter, where Priceline gets many of the tickets that are sold though its site. The airlines prefer to keep control of their own discounting channels to the extent possible, but their main objection to Priceline today is the message that all seats are commodities and the carrier matters less than the cost. That is precisely the type of commoditization that airlines spend billions annually in advertising to avoid.

The airline industry itself, of course, provides a familiar example of a sophisticated dynamic pricing system that is totally compatible with today's business models. Dynamic pricing has in fact made it possible for airlines to fill the maximum number of plane seats at the most favorable prices. The airline pricing algorithms require massive back-end computing power and an expensive dedicated computer reservation system. But despite the high cost of implementation and maintenance, this dynamic pricing model has contributed considerably to the industry's profitability.

The prices, however, are fully controlled by the airlines, and the information that is available is typically too complicated to be very useful. Consumers and business buyers can try to outsmart the pricing model from the outside, but they don't have a way to get any leverage inside of the system.

In addition to Priceline, there are now many Web sites that offer last-minute airfare discounts and special limited low prices, so that the consumer can find out at least a better range of price options. But unlike the research that a consumer may do on a stable-priced good such as a new car, the open information pool stops at the boundary of the computer reservation system.

Imagine if consumers could penetrate the reservation systems and watch the movements of supply and demand for airline tickets as easily as they can track the bids on the stock market. They could choose to buy their tickets at an early stage, when average prices were high, or take a chance that price levels would decline closer to the departure date. An alert service would keep them informed of any flurry of activity that might indicate price movement, so that they could grab a seat before demand overtook supply. Sometimes, consumers would get a great deal and other times, when flights were in demand, the airline would be a big winner. But the market would decide openly, based on shared information. This would indeed be a disruptive model for today's businesses. Once the information behind the pricing becomes visible, and the opportunity exists to act on that heretofore hidden information, companies have to adjust to a completely different market dynamic. Despite all the publicity about Priceline and other consumer-blind dynamic pricing systems, that transformation is still waiting in the wings.

Hambrecht's creation of an open market for investors in IPO shares illustrates why this next stage of disruption must be based on more open information access. William R. Hambrecht, well-known investment banker and cofounder of the enormously successful Hambrecht & Quist investment bank, left his job at the beginning of 1998 to start up a new venture. His goal was simple: "To allow broader investment in the IPO process by small institutional investors and the average individual."[5]

According to Hambrecht, the Internet is the only way to effectively reach hundreds of thousands of investors and to pool their interest at a given time to create an IPO with a broad base of small investments. He recalls that while he was still at H&Q, he kept asking his own staff if the Net wasn't ultimately a threat to them and the establishment in investment banking. But the answer was always negative, reflecting the problem with trying to initiate radical change from inside established organizations, even ones in the eye of the Internet storm.

Hambrecht finally decided that it was time to do something very different in order to change the model for taking companies public. The model for his new company, an electronic investment bank called OpenIPO, is Net-based and Web-centric.

Hambrecht wanted to break the mold of the traditional IPO by avoiding the pattern of a low initial offer price followed by a huge spike in the price during the first day of trading and then a steep price decline toward the initial offer level. This pattern provided lucrative financial returns to insider and institutional investors who were in a position to buy at the offer price and then sell quickly before any declines, but it penalized the individual investor who couldn't get access to shares until they had already peaked in price.

To the extent that the share value rose quickly over the initial offering price, it also meant that the initial offer price could have been higher and that the company itself did not get full benefit of the market's demand for its shares. Creating an environment where the initial share price was pegged more accurately to the actual market demand for the stock was a challenge that Hambrecht was determined to solve. The best way to do this, he decided, was to be sure that the potential investors were well informed in advance of the offering, with access to the type of background information that large investment banks shared only with their institutional clients. Once everyone had done the research necessary to decide how much they wanted to pay for this

particular stock, Hambrecht would set up a bidding process to allo-
cate the stock to investors based on the balance of price and demand.

OpenIPO uses a Dutch auction model based on bidders putting in
their highest price and number of shares; no matter how high the bids
are, everyone gets the same price as the clearing price. Hambrecht
feels strongly that even though it may result in a higher average opening price than the traditional IPO model, the bid system protects the
buyers and keeps them coming back. This is based on his conviction
that markets work properly only if information is distributed fairly
and equitably to all. He notes that it took almost thirty years for fixed
rate broker commissions to decline, while the Internet created a climate for individual online trading in just three years. Now brokers
have to come to terms with open information and pricing systems
where small investors get as much information as the large players.
Hambrecht sees OpenIPO as enabling this inevitable transition to
stock market openness, because there is a huge pent up demand for
early access to IPO shares.[6]

By increasing the amount of information available to individual
buyers, consumer-oriented e-markets of all types are changing the
way we think about pricing. But these new markets are still in formation and are likely to run parallel to traditional consumer channels
for the foreseeable future. The pace of change and the potential for
disruption are much stronger in the business-to-business arena.

Business-to-Business Auctions

From commodity markets to surplus inventory auctions, the auction exchange has a long history in company-to-company dealings. In
many cases, moving such auctions to the Web is truly a simple and
vastly more efficient substitution for a familiar fax- or telephone-
based activity. That helps to explain why the spectrum of business-to-
business online auction activity is extensive and why more than two
hundred B2B auction companies opened for business in 1999 alone.
New market entrants, no matter what industry they are joining, benefit from the spread of dynamic pricing and e-marketplaces because

establishing a pricing range for new products is one of the most difficult things to accomplish effectively in a static-pricing environment. For this reason, small companies and especially Internet start-ups are typically quicker to see the positive side of auctions and they are ready to tightly integrate auction tools into their sales strategies and product offerings.

The swarm of online activity around surplus inventory auctions in a variety of industries barely registers on the disruption scale, except for those brokers who used to handle this by phone and personal contacts and who are getting a quick lesson in Internet time and the meaning of disintermediation. Surplus goods are starting to turn over more quickly and to fetch better prices in the more popular online auctions, but the overall economic impact is still not significant.

The small business market, 7 million strong in the United States alone and historically very difficult to aggregate, has disruptive potential if the majority of small company managers become regular participants in the brokered economy. Typically, these buyers have been quite localized and have not had access to convenient auction services or the time to investigate best price options. BizBuyer is one of the dozens of Internet start-ups betting that they have the formula to convert small businesses to dynamic pricing portals. BizBuyer is set up to facilitate reverse auctions, letting the small business owner specify the type of goods or services desired via the Web and then mailing the request to preregistered vendors who are the best matches. The bids come into the BizBuyer site, and the five best responses are forwarded to the buyer in the form of a comparative Web page. It's up to the small business owner to make the final selection and consummate the deal.

The goal is to get the best price for the least amount of effort, and BizBuyer is getting good reviews from early users. With more than 6,000 vendors already participating and more than 10,000 active bids in the pipeline at the end of 1999, the company was over the first hump of attracting initial critical mass. The quest for all Internet companies is to get big fast, but this is especially important for an auction exchange where increased numbers bring better value to all participants.

BizBuyer is aiming to top 100,000 registered users by the end of 2000 and accelerate from there to millions of bids per year. If that happens, the ripples of disruption in the small business marketplace will start to turn to waves. One harbinger of success—and of the potential for broad impact—is the fact that eBay CEO Meg Whitman is a BizBuyer investor and board member. Whitman's involvement and support is a good indication that the small business auction market is destined to make its mark on the Web.

All exchanges require a critical mass of participants to achieve liquidity, and the more items that are offered for sale, the more likely it is that any individual buyer will have a greater choice in selecting and negotiating for the perfect match. On the seller side, a continuous flow of potential buyers and bidders increases the chance for rapid turnover. So it is essential to attract both buyers and sellers into the electronic marketplace, and the company that manages to capture a critical mass will have a commanding first-mover advantage. Conversely, the marketplace that comes in second will have to work particularly hard to overcome a slow start. There is a natural monopoly in effect in focused aggregation that makes life very difficult for latecomer wannabes.

Commerce One and Ariba Software, two of the leading competitors in selling software for setting up business-to-business exchanges, are thus understandably reluctant to lose ground in providing core services to their customers. So it is no surprise that both companies scrambled to acquire dynamic pricing and auction capabilities within a few weeks of each other or that both companies decided to buy up existing players rather than take the time to build dynamic pricing engines from scratch.

These two are far from the only providers on online procurement services. Long-established leaders such as General Electric and IBM are among the many large corporations starting to pay more attention to this area. Regardless of who ultimately wins the lion's market share of multinational business-to-business dynamic pricing, the simultaneous entry of Commerce One and Ariba into the fray is an indication of things to come. Both of these companies have impressive client lists that include the big three auto manufacturers and more than half of the Fortune 500 companies. With all these giants auction-enabled, the probability of disruptive change moves noticeably toward one. The sheer weight of the money being spent among the Commerce One and Ariba clients will make significant waves once it begins to shift to purchasing via online auctions.

To sum up the movement toward widespread availability of dynamic pricing, it is useful to recap the potential benefits for both sellers and buyers in this environment. The seller benefits are as follows:

- access to a broader buyer group and new markets;
- establishment of clear market price points;
- transaction speed;
- rapid turnover of inventory;
- direct feedback market research; and
- the opportunity to establish customer relationships and provide follow on services and offers to bidders.

Buyer benefits include the following:

- the ability to determine price points on a transaction-by-transaction basis;
- the accessibility of information about popularity or scarcity of product;
- the ability to be proactive (issue request) as well as reactive (place bids);
- increased choice; and
- lower prices.

Even though the summary of seller advantages is impressive, there is typically more resistance on the part of established sellers to join in a dynamic exchange than there is on the part of buyers. As Payton Anderson, founder of SciQuest noted about wooing suppliers to participate in open information sites on the Web, there is definitely a reluctance to give up proprietary advantages and fixed-price profits as well as to incur the expense involved in revamping house systems and pricing strategies. But the risk of not being represented at all at the most important markets outweighs the downside of head-to-head competition. If dynamic pricing becomes the major way to move their goods, the suppliers will have to be there, just the way they had to come to terms with doing business via the Internet several years ago.

Those that are smart will be looking to establish a full-fledged digital value system framework with their key customers that can absorb the dynamic pricing component as needed. And they will also figure out how to use the information released from the open bidding model to make their core businesses more flexible and action-oriented. This will put them in an excellent position to make the most of the spread of auction markets.

Setting a Dynamic Price

Clearly, the Internet has been a powerful force for shifting the balance toward dynamic pricing in the B2B and consumer realms. Auctions grab the headlines, especially in the consumer domain. But as we have seen, the consumer-to-consumer move to auction markets is not nearly as significant as the business-to-business move toward online dynamic pricing of goods and services. Opportunities abound in every industry and type of service, as the Internet makes it essential to get customer feedback and buy-in to new offers.

Bank One Vice President Dick Vos, for example, can see an application for dynamic pricing in the traditionally stable-price precincts of commercial banking. He points out that the other departments of the bank clearly have brokerage skills in order to manage investment services, but the organization hasn't yet figured out how to transfer those skills to the whole organization. But offering Bank One commercial customers dynamic pricing options would actually help the bank set realistic prices for the value-added services and products they provide. This approach could solve the frustrating chicken-and-egg problem of wanting to add innovative online services but not wanting to increase the basic charges to the customer. Vos notes that it is already difficult to get customers to pay higher prices for something that looks similar to the service now available to them for free—especially after training them to expect that online services mean cost savings all around. By creating dynamic pricing options for bundles of new services, the Bank would develop a better sense of how customers valued their offers and what types of services generated the most demand.

Like many large corporations, Bank One currently has to rely on time-consuming and imprecise methods for pricing new products and services. This task is especially challenging for Internet-based services where there may not be anything comparable out in the marketplace. Companies may hire a pricing consultant or set up a series of focus groups to test the waters, but these measures at best narrow the range to a more accurate guesstimate. As with an IPO, until the product hits the market, there is no reliable way to predetermine if the price is at the right level. By the time companies get enough feedback to understand if they have missed the mark, it is usually too late to make any significant changes. Unlike with an IPO, the pain of product mispricing does not abate quickly but metastasizes into a long-term headache.

Vos notes that despite all this time and expense, it may be impossible to come up with the single best pricing structure. In fact it may well be that there is no one price that will suit all customers at all times. Inside a brokered economy, there would not have to be a single price point. With brokered services, customers could purchase exactly what they needed at any moment—and the price they paid would reflect the current value to them as individual customers. Finding out the value of the service, Vos concludes, would be especially important as the Bank begins to roll out more online products to more diverse groups of clients. Being able to harvest the information about how a particular service was used when the price was market-driven would initially be at least as valuable as whatever the revenue itself turned out to be. Despite these theoretical advantages to dynamic pricing, Vos acknowledges that the move to fully brokered services is still in the future for Bank One and for the banking industry at large.[7]

Bank One may not be in a position to implement brokered pricing across its commercial division, but Vos has captured the essential value proposition of the brokered economy—position yourself to turn the information about dynamic pricing into a new form of value. The rise of e-marketplaces means that companies will have to develop a fundamentally different approach to pricing, distribution channels, and obtaining the supplies needed for their own production requirements. The progression of information sharing leading to action and becoming more valuable in the process that we saw unfold in chapter 4 now also extends into the pricing process as well.

Within a digital value system, companies will able to move to dynamic pricing in the context of trusted relationships and clusters of services built into each other's business processes. This limits the disruptive impact of dynamic pricing while increasing its positive effect on the marketplace as a whole. The cost to provide goods and services is likely to decline, thanks to effective use of dynamic pricing on the supply side. But that cost will be more likely to fluctuate than ever before, and the ability to obtain goods and services will be the critical factor in whether or not a company can supply its own customers effectively. Everyone will be even more dependent on everyone else, driving higher marketplace participation since the critical goods will be available only through these markets.

Conclusion

Long before the Internet era, markets brought hopeful sellers and potential buyers together in a framework that facilitated efficient information exchange. The farmer made the effort to pack up his beans and his pigs and lug them to the village square because that was where the greatest number of potential buyers could find out the most information about his offer in the shortest period of time. And he could keep an eye on the ebb and flow of other sales to determine how many pigs were available that month and how they compared to his.

Once information about the goods could travel independently from the items themselves, the physical presence of the goods was less important than providing a sufficient number of buyers and sellers with enough information in a timely enough way to facilitate action. So marketplaces became information exchanges, and buyers and sellers delegated their authority to make purchase decisions to trusted brokers. Pig bellies and soybean futures are still traded on commodity markets, but now the trading takes place in front of giant computer screens that feed information of all sorts from around the world to be summed up in a single ask/bid transaction.

It would, however, be myopic to conclude that the long history of physical and electronic marketplaces is simply being replicated on the Internet. The spread of digital dynamic pricing is different in kind as well as in scale. Every type of good and service is going to be impacted, from the most mundane to the most rare and expensive. As every industry sector moves to an online marketplace where value is dynamically determined, it becomes inevitable that fixed pricing will in fact give way to value-based pricing.

Pockets of fixed prices will certainly persist, and since many of them will be in places that are highly visible to the mass market—such as retail bricks-and-mortar stores—the depth of the transformation may not dawn on the average consumer for quite some time. But behind the scenes, the pressure for real-time market-based adjustments in price for business-to-business goods will prevail.

Once dynamic pricing spreads to the majority of transactions, companies must be prepared to change their orientation to the marketplace and their own internal systems to accommodate it. Establishing a continuum between e-sourcing and e-pricing will be vital. Companies must be able to manage a constant stream of information about changes in price, availability, and demand for goods and services and will themselves become brokers in allocating products among their suppliers and customers.

CHAPTER NINE

Maximum Digital Value

Unchained Value proposes a new strategic framework for organizing business relationships and processes, an approach that springs from the realities of the online world. The Internet's explosive growth and the astronomical market valuation of online companies over the past few years have propelled some shaky business models to prominence. But long-term success in the Internet economy requires mastery of networked business processes that go a lot deeper than today's popularity contests. Companies must become adept at turning complex information into action, at building trusted relationships that can transform quantity into quality, and at delivering targeted, customized services whenever and wherever they are needed. What's more, they must find ways to connect these activities to their customers and business partners to ensure that the collaborative pooling of information that is the life force of the digital value system continues to flow freely in all directions.

Precisely because it involves interplay among multiple participants in a constantly changing pattern, generating sustainable digital value is a formidable challenge in itself. Looking out for the well-being of partners and customers in more than rhetorical terms is an unaccustomed, and sometimes uncomfortable, responsibility. Managers are tempted to give nontangible results, such as building fully interactive relationships, short shrift in the rush to make quarterly numbers. But these are the short cuts that lead away from the collaborative center of value and that cut companies off from their most important assets—the information and trust of partners and customers. On the Internet, if you cross the finish line alone, you lose.

Subscribing to a strategy based on shared information and trust does not mean that competition and efficient execution go out the door. On the contrary, companies that recognize information sharing as essential to efficiency and scale on the Internet will be in a position to transform that information into action most decisively and will set the competitive pace. These are the companies that will be in tune with the ever-faster cycles of online technology adoption and shifts in market demand.

The progression from simply doing business on the Internet to launching a digital value system is not automatic, however. It requires companies to reevaluate their overall strategy, the integration of network applications throughout the organization, and their relationships with supply and distribution channels, business partners, customers, and competitors. Whether they work in established corporations or Internet ventures, managers have two compelling reasons for making a sweeping change. First, the focus on digital value breaks the now artificial barriers that separate processes inside the firm from those taking place in the global electronic marketplace. The Internet has already disrupted every firm's internal processes by introducing so many options, information sources, and service providers that cannot be controlled inside the boundaries of the firm. Clinging to current practices and struggling to keep internal processes under control using established systems have become distractions and a losing battle. Second and more important, the digital value framework turns customers into contributing partners in growing the enterprise. Internet users are demanding a level of immediate gratification and customized service that can be delivered only when they are admitted to the inner circle.

Companies can't afford to cater to millions of individual decision makers by using old models of customer relationship management. But making customers into active partners and beneficiaries of shared digital value unlocks the limits to growth.

The transformation starts, as we have seen, with recognizing the limits of the traditional value chain view of business processes and focusing on different types of core activities that are essential to create business value and generate increasing returns in an Internet economy—information, trust, relationships, and services.

The Internet sets no limits on size or speed. Software spreads to millions of desktops in just a few months. Ideas turn into products overnight. But it doesn't happen in isolation. The power of the Internet is in its connections. We have seen how the strategic value of connections between information, trust, relationships, and services can multiply as more and more participants join a digital value system. This cycle of increasing value attracts more partners and creates a deeper and richer pool of resources, all connected to each other through the information and action that they trigger.

Once it moves online, the information that a product or service generates—not the specific item being fabricated, delivered, or serviced—becomes the source of sustainable value. When traditional value chains are linked up to the Internet without a change in strategy, companies are hard-pressed to keep up with the torrent of information generated by diverse inputs, from production lines to EDI to the tracking of Web site visits. Managers need a digital value framework to turn this information into action that can be transmitted back across the value system. In the business-to-business world this leads to formation of online exchanges and e-marketplaces where buying and selling agreements that used to be limited to "pair-wise" agreements between companies are concluded in an open, real-time environment. Transforming partnerships and business-to-business exchanges into action-oriented insights requires information pooling among all participants. Then this information must be synchronized with data coming from online customers and outsourcing and fulfillment partners. Managers can then concentrate on which types of changes and ripples in the information pool are significant and quickly turn those observations into action by interacting directly with the internal and external parts of the system as an integrated whole.

The digital trust hierarchy provides a needed avenue for involving individual customers directly in this new form of information sharing and mutual value. Understanding and respecting the differences between business and consumer motivation to share information online are essential in building individual trust. Making a clear covenant with customers about how and when their information is going to be used creates the foundation for active personalization that reflects what really matters to a particular individual. Once customers buy into active information sharing, they are also willing to participate in making the feedback loop richer for all and may even see the value of information pooling, especially when it is clear that they will also benefit from the results. At the top of the trust hierarchy, when the customer is actively participating in the information collection, new forms of service can create lasting customer loyalty and lifetime revenues. At this point, companies are much better able to listen and respond to the different types of customers as individuals, setting the stage for customer-initiated and customer-maintained segmentation of services and products. This level of engagement adds value to the whole collective of users and business partners.

A fundamental breakthrough of the Internet is allowing companies to harvest the power of exponential relationships. Once they have laid the groundwork for real-time information management and two-way trust, companies are able to handle increasing numbers of customers and interactions without losing any quality in terms of the individual responsiveness. In fact, they are at the point where "more is better" and they actually can improve the products and services that they offer as more and more people start to participate. These exponential relationships grow more powerful and satisfying the more people get to interact with each other and get access to the insights or the cost savings and financial benefits of a shared pool of information.

The transition to e-services allows companies to build new value into product offerings. The value of the information, trust, and relationships that companies have developed with customers can now be extended into different types of services that attach to even commodity products. Once companies are able to capture the information and the trust and manage relationships effectively, it becomes possible to turn every interaction and sale into a potential service. In this context the brokered economy becomes an efficient market mechanism to move goods—both on the purchasing and the sales side—at prices that are validated in real time by market demand. What might be lost on higher margins can be more than balanced by the efficiencies of getting such rapid response to new products and services. Companies will be able to get an instant reading of the value of their latest thinking and be able to adjust it and fine-tune the value-added aspects with direct market responses. We no longer look at a toaster as a dumb appliance, because we have seen how the digital value system can link that toaster and countless other commodity products to a vast demand for online services that provide new and higher margin revenue streams. Even more important, these services connect deeply with customer needs and thus create a level of loyalty that cannot be achieved by products alone.

E-services also transform the economics of market entry in all industries. The potential to access business process and distribution services as needed means that smaller companies on the Web can afford to buy best-of-breed IT and logistical services in small slices on a "pay-as-you-go" basis. Recognizing that there are new market and revenue possibilities created by distributing these services over the Internet, large companies are rushing to transform their own products into Internet-connected ASP offerings.

Connecting to the Future

The digital value framework provides managers with a coherent approach to Internet strategy and new ways to generate value in the global electronic marketplace. But the implementations of digital value don't end with today's online environment of Internet-connected personal computers and Web pages. This framework provides vital preparation for the next stage of business transformation. No matter how much impact the Web has had on how we buy, sell, market, and service products, it is not the end state of the Internet revolution. Managers must be prepared for another transfer of their value proposition to the next generation of marketplace interconnections and digital communication.

We are already seeing an explosion of investment in mobile commerce, as companies and customers begin using wireless connections to the Internet through personal digital assistants and cell phones. With projections that one billion digital wireless phones will be deployed around the world by 2004, it is not too early to develop a mobile commerce program that builds on the lessons of the Web era. Companies cannot count on simply translating the strategies and products that have been successful Web-based offerings into this new commerce arena. Customers will expect different types of service, support, and value from their mobile phones and PDAs. Instead of helping themselves by surfing the Web, they will need individualized, location-sensitive responses. The digital value framework will become even more important in the mobile environment, where trust and information pooling will be able to produce high-value services and where there will be less opportunity for entry as customers gravitate to a few trusted service providers.

Reaching for maximum value in the Internet economy means moving beyond today's enterprise-centered strategies. To survive the churn, the competition, and even their own short-term successes on the Net, companies must redefine their goals from competitive advantage into collaborative advantage. That means giving away value now—to customers and partners and even competitors—in order to reap increasing value later. It means putting trust before technology, and investing in relationships as the foundation for future services. The race to establish a clear value proposition for mobile commerce will once again match the resources of established, multinational companies against those of Internet-based start-ups, and the winners will be those firms that enter the race with a digital value system already in place. The companies that establish close and trusted relationships early in this race will capture a new degree of customer loyalty with every customer interaction that will prove very difficult to dislodge. In fact, they will be well along the road to achieving maximum digital value.

Notes

Chapter 1

1. Ernst & Young, "The Second Annual Internet Shopping Study," www.ey.com, January 1999.
2. Louis V. Gerstner, Jr., "Blinded By Dot-Com Alchemy," *Business Week*, 27 March 2000, 40.
3. Laura Rohde, "Gartner: Expect three-quarters of e-projects to flop," *Computerworld*, online edition,www.computerworld.com, 24 September 1999.
4. Katrina Brooker, "Amazon vs. Everybody," *Fortune*, 8 November 1999, 128.

Chapter 2

1. Michael Porter, *Competitive Advantage* (New York: Free Press, 1985), 36.
2. Ibid., 39–40.
3. Mary Cronin, *Doing Business on the Internet* (New York: Van Nostrand Reinhold, 1994).
4. Jeffrey F. Rayport and John Sviokla, "Managing in the Marketspace," *Harvard Business Review* 72 (November–December 1994): 141–150.
5. Albert Pang, "Internet Commerce Procurement Application Market Review, Forecast, and User Trends, 1998–2003," IDC, www.idc.com, August 1999.
6. Amy Doan, "Palm Flop," *Forbes*, online edition, www.forbes.com, 29 November 1999.
7. Handspring Web site, www.handspring.com, November 1999.
8. Original background information on eCoverage was obtained from David Coulter, Partner, The Beacon Group, USA, an eCoverage investor, and board member, from a personal conversation with the author and from his

presentation "Some Experiences in the New Economy" at the conference "The Impact of the Global Information Revolution on International Management," sponsored by the Carnegie Bosch Institute for Applied Studies in International Management, October 21–23, 1999.

9. Scott Woolley, "A Car Dealer By Any Other Name," *Forbes*, online edition, www.forbes.com, 29 November, 1999.

Chapter 3

1. "The dot.com within Ford," *US News & World Report*, 7 February 2000, 34.
2. "Yahoo Still Swinging Single," *Wired News*, online edition, www.wired news.com, 25 September 1999.
3. Carclub.com, "Carclub.com Teams Up with eBay to Provide Automotive Services for eBay Users" (press release, 3 August 1999), www.carclub.com.

Chapter 4

1. Claude E. Shannon, "A Mathematical Theory of Communication," *Bell System Technical Journal* 27 (July 1948): 379–423; and (October 1948): 623–656.
2. "The World in 1999," *The Economist*, December 1999, 96.
3. Raymond Lane, opening address, Carnegie Bosch Institute's conference, "The Impact of the Global Information Revolution on International Management," San Francisco, CA, October 22, 1999.
4. www.dell.com.
5. Payton Anderson, interview by author, Raleigh, NC, 13 August 1999.
6. Manoj George, interview by author, Durham, NC, 12 August 1999.
7. Christopher MacAskill, telephone interview by author, 15 December 1999.

Chapter 5

1. The European Union has adopted much stronger privacy protection measures than the United States. These are mandated in "The European Directive on Data Protection." See www.europarl.eu.int/dg2/hearings/20000222/ibe/links/en/default.htm.
2. Lorrie F. Cranor et al., "Beyond Concern: Understanding Net Users' Attitudes About Online Privacy," www.research.att.com/projects/privacystudy, 14 April 1999.
3. The diagram in figure 5-1 has obvious parallels to Abraham Maslow's Hierarchy of Needs, which postulates that humans cannot achieve self-actualization until their basic physical and emotional needs have been met. The idea of moving though a required step-by-step progression where the early steps are preconditions for achieving a higher level has been applied to other areas as well. It is particularly useful in the case of digital trust because it

clarifies the relationship of security and Web design to the more advanced requirements for ongoing trusted interactions.
4. Cheskin Research, Studio Archetype, and Sapient, "E-Commerce Trust Study," www.sapient.com/cheskin.
5. Polly Sprenger, "Sun on Privacy: 'Get Over It,'" *Wired News*, online edition, www.wirednews.com, 26 January 1999.
6. The Online Privacy Alliance, Guidelines for Online Privacy Policies, www.privacyalliance.org/resources/ppguidelines.shtml.
7. Federal Trade Commission, "Self Regulation and Privacy On-line: A Report to Congress," July 1999.
8. This incident was first reported by Richard Smith and is detailed on his web site at www.tiac.net/users/smiths/privacy.
9. This discussion of Napster is intended to illustrate the potential for exponential relationships that are formed on the Internet and does not consider the legal issues associated with downloading and sharing digital music files. It should be noted that Napster's role in encouraging such activities has been criticized by many established recording labels and artists and that the Recording Industry Association of America filed a suit against Napster in 1999.

Chapter 6
1. Michael Lewis, *The New New Thing: A Silicon Valley Story* (New York: Norton, 1999).
2. Stacy Lawrence, "E-commerce Deficiencies," www.iconocast.com, 28 October 1999.
3. Ian Suttcliffe, telephone interview by author, 15 November 1999 and 25 May 2000.
4. Mediconsult.com, "Visitor Bill of Rights," www.mediconsult.com, June 2000. Reprinted with permission.
5. Suttcliffe, telephone interview by author.
6. Clayton Christensen, *The Innovator's Dilemma* (Boston: Harvard Business School Press, 1997), 103.
7. Peter Drucker, *Management Challenges for the 21st Century* (New York: HarperBusiness, 1999), 28.

Chapter 7
1. Carly Fiorina , keynote address at 1999 Comdex conference, Las Vegas, NV, November 15, 1999, www.hp.com/ghp/ceo/speeches/comdex99_full.html.
2. Boston Consulting Group and shop.org, "The State of Online Retailing 3.0," www.bcg.com, April 1999.

3. Intuit "Intuit Opens QuickBooks Internet Gateway to Offer E-Services to Millions of Small Businesses" (press release, 20 October 1999), www.intuit.com.

4. Phil Gibson, telephone interview by author, October 1999.

5. Kevin Werbach, "Now in Syndication," *Red Herring*, November 1999, 160.

6. Fiorina, keynote address at 1999 Comdex conference.

Chapter 8

1. Kip Frey, interview by author, Durham, NC, August 1999.

2. Matthew Nelson, "Moai CEO Dissects Online Auctions," *InfoWorld Electric*, www.infoworld.com, 26 April 1999.

3. Steven J. Kafka, "eMarketplaces Boost B2B Trade," *The Forrester Report*, February 2000.

4. Vernon Keenan, "Exchanges in the Internet Economy," *The Keenan Report*, www.keenanvision.com, 26 October 1998.

5. W. R. Hambrecht, keynote speech, Carnegie Bosch Institute's conference, "The Impact of the Global Information Revolution on International Management," San Francisco, CA, October 22, 1999.

6. Ibid.

7. Richard Vos, telephone interview by author, July 1999.

Index

About the Author

MARY J. CRONIN, Ph.D., is Professor of Management at Boston College and focuses her research on the development and implementation of e-business strategies. She teaches courses in strategy, electronic commerce, and international information management. Dr. Cronin also works as a consultant with Fortune 500 and multinational corporations and serves on the board of several Internet-based start-ups and a venture capital fund. Her work as a speaker, consultant, and author illustrates how the Internet is transforming business processes and competitive opportunities within industries.

Dr. Cronin's books include *Doing Business on the Internet: How the Electronic Highway Is Transforming America, Global Advantage on the Internet, The Internet Strategy Handbook: Lessons from the New Frontier of Business,* and *Banking and Finance on the Internet.* She also wrote the chapter "Privacy and Electronic Commerce" for the book *Public Policy and the Internet,* published by the Hoover Institution, and is the coauthor of *Branding the Future,* to be published in 2001. In addition, she has published numerous articles and case studies on electronic commerce.